£20

*Dennstaedtia punctilobula*
hay-scented fern

# A NATURAL BALANCE

The K.C. Irving Environmental Science Centre
and Harriet Irving Botanical Gardens
at Acadia University

*2 2 / 9 / 2 2*

ALEX NOVELL and JOHN LEROUX

The K.C. Irving Environmental Science Centre and Harriet Irving Botanical Gardens

Acadia University

*£20*

Edited by Paula Sarson.
Jacket and page design by Julie Scriver with John Leroux.
Printed in Canada by Friesens.
10 9 8 7 6 5 4 3 2 1

Library and Archives Canada Cataloguing in Publication

Title: A natural balance : the K.C. Irving Environmental Science Centre and Harriet Irving
Botanical Gardens at Acadia University / Alex Novell and John Leroux.
Other titles: K.C. Irving Environmental Science Centre and Harriet Irving Botanical Gardens at Acadia University
Names: Novell, Alex, author. | Leroux, John, 1970- author.
Identifiers: Canadiana 20210181087 | ISBN 9781777663209 (hardcover)
Subjects: LCSH: K.C. Irving Environmental Science Centre—History. | LCSH: Harriet Irving Botanical Gardens—History. |
LCSH: K.C. Irving Environmental Science Centre—Pictorial works. | LCSH: Harriet Irving Botanical Gardens—Pictorial works. |
LCSH: College science museums—Nova Scotia—Wolfville—Design and construction. | LCSH: Botanical gardens—Nova Scotia—
Wolfville—Design and construction. | LCSH: Architecture—Nova Scotia—Wolfville. | LCSH: Plants—Maritime Provinces. |
LCSH: Trees—Maritime Provinces. | LCSH: Wolfville (N.S.)—Buildings, structures, etc.
Classification: LCC NA747.W65 N68 2021 | DDC 720.9716/34—dc23

Acadia University is located in Mi'kma'ki, the ancestral territory of the Mi'kmaq People.

Published by
The K.C. Irving Environmental Science Centre and
Harriet Irving Botanical Gardens, Acadia University
15 University Avenue
Wolfville, NS
CANADA B4P 2R6
kcirvingcentre.acadiau.ca

*As an Acadia student, I am so fortunate to have access to such a beautiful facility as the K.C. Irving Environmental Science Centre and Harriet Irving Botanical Gardens. I have spent many long afternoons in the Garden Room, close to the fireplace, revising notes and basking in the calmness of the space. With its large windows and warm colours, it is by far my favourite place to study on campus.*

*It is inspiring to walk past the conservatory and greenhouse rooms to see the research of my fellow students. I was also lucky enough to have an entire course in the Harriet Irving Gardens. It was a wonderful experience to be outside as the trails, plants, and living creatures were incorporated into our classes. The Centre and Gardens are an incredible resource for all students at Acadia University. I couldn't imagine Acadia without it.*

— SARAH LAVALLÉE, Arthur Irving Scholar, Acadia class of 2022

*Icterus galbula*
Baltimore oriole

# Foreword

Today is my ninetieth birthday. Looking across the Bay of Fundy to neighbouring Nova Scotia, I think about all the visits I've made to Acadia University over the years, and I've enjoyed every one. In my role as chancellor for fourteen years, many visits were for graduations, but many were for all the planning, time, thought, and hard work we put into our gift to Acadia University of the K.C. Irving Environmental Science Centre and the Harriet Irving Botanical Gardens, named in honour of our parents.

The road to Wolfville, Nova Scotia, is one my father K.C. Irving travelled in 1917 to attend Acadia, and I would follow some thirty years later, after my brother Jim and before my brother Jack. My memories are of happy student days, playing rugby, and the important lessons of teamwork. It is there where I met many lifelong friends who were my inspiration in the creation of the Garden Room of the K.C. Irving Centre as a place where friends meet.

The story of Acadia University in our family is long and meaningful. In 1996, it was an honour to be asked to serve as chancellor of Acadia. My heartfelt commitment to take on the role was because I wanted to do something for the students. I hope you will think about this when you go through these pages. You will see how this special place enhances students' lives in so many ways: in their academic pursuits, appreciation of nature, and time together with classmates, friends, family, and the greater community.

There is no real measure of the time and thought that went into the creation of such a place, but this important story written by Alex Novell and John Leroux will give you cause to ponder and will provide some insight. Thank you to Alex and John most sincerely for this story. Alex is a wonderful friend who was with us from the earliest thought of what we envisaged for such a place. What he created at the Harriet Irving Botanical Gardens, and what architect Robert Stern and his associates Graham Wyatt and Preston Gumberich accomplished at the K.C. Irving Environmental Science Centre, is truly a masterpiece. They have left their mark on history. They worked with my good friend Hans Klohn and me in a solid commitment to quality every step of the way. Before he died on April 15, 2020, Hans always wore his K.C. Irving Environmental Science Centre pin on his lapel. Hans is remembered for his loyalty.

When I visit Acadia, I always look forward to walking in the gardens. They are a beautiful place of happiness, peace, and knowledge. And when I visit the K.C. Irving Environmental Science Centre, I am reminded of the outstanding artistry, skill, and workmanship of many local artisans—and I am proud of them.

Dr. Kelvin Ogilvie, former president of Acadia, was very much part of our vision. His unwavering support, travelling all those miles with us, near and far, collecting ideas, and his hard work in putting all the important pieces together for the building to have a strong academic mission as well as a social purpose are the important building blocks and an integral part of the foundation.

Arthur, Sarah, and Sandra Irving

Former president Ray Ivany often says (so kindly) how everything about the K.C. Irving Environmental Science Centre helps define Acadia in making it stand out above the rest. Today's president Peter Ricketts echoes these sentiments. He and his team are always working hard to use this important resource as a standout feature of the Acadia community. There are so many other individuals who were the builders and the keepers and who are kindly mentioned in the acknowledgements. I thank them all most sincerely.

Sandra and Sarah work closely with me in most of the things I take on in life. They were always by my side in all the graduations I presided over as Chancellor. Sandra put her heart into every detail on the project, and I thank her very much. We have walked all the paths in the garden many times, and we know many of the plants and flowers by name. When we stop to admire the impressive features of the Centre, we are reminded that we put our heart and soul into choosing each one.

My thoughts on the plaque in the Garden Room are ones I leave you with: *Enjoy your stay at Acadia—Time passes very quickly.*

ARTHUR IRVING
July 14, 2020

*Arctostaphylos uva-ursi*
common bearberry

# A Master Plan

*The K.C. Irving Environmental Science Centre*
*and Harriet Irving Botanical Gardens*

## ALEX NOVELL

I must confess that I am not much of a horticulturist. Interesting though it may be to the dedicated gardener, I cannot warm to the Victorian obsession with collecting plants from disparate ecosystems and displaying them together without any connection to their natural context. The most beautiful collection of flowers I have ever seen was pretty much wild. It resides in an alpine valley on the French-Italian border, with a clear mountain stream and a myriad of miniature gardens adapted to each of a wide variety of habitats: high meadow, rocky mountainside, lake margin, marsh and bog, streamside, forest and wooded glade, ranging from snow-covered uplands to lush lower pastures. They are at their loveliest for a short season in June, and nothing a designer could conceive could come close to such abundance and beauty.

And so it was that when Arthur Irving began to talk to me about the possibility of creating a garden at Acadia University, Wolfville, Nova Scotia, in memory of his mother, Harriet, who loved flowers (1), I was excited to learn that he had in mind something that would celebrate the natural flora of the part of Canada the family grew up in and explored together. Here was an opportunity to show the richness and diversity of the wild flowering plants of this region, not simply by collecting and displaying them by their taxonomic classification or some such scientific artifice, but in their natural plant associations in habitat as close to nature as we could artfully craft.

A botanical garden should be more than a repository of plants. It is first and foremost for people to enjoy (2), to appreciate the vegetation and the wildlife it attracts (3, 4), and to provide an opportunity for learning and for serious research. Arthur understood this, but he wanted to do something more for the students of the university that he, his father, his brothers Jim and Jack, and his wife Sandra had attended. He aspired to give them a building of their own both for study and for quiet relaxation. Add to this Sandra Irving's desire that the teaching and research facilities should be of the highest possible standard, and the K.C. Irving Environmental Science Centre and Harriet Irving Botanical Gardens project was born. It took nearly three years to research and design, and a further two years to

build. Now, twenty years after its completion, it is maturing and being nurtured by a dedicated team under the direction of head gardener Melanie Priesnitz.

This is the story of how it was created.

## The Acadian Forest Region

Acadia University lies in the Annapolis Valley in a distinctive, temperate broad-leaf and mixed-woodland region that includes southern Quebec, Nova Scotia, New Brunswick, and Prince Edward Island. It also encompasses much of New England: northern Maine, parts of New Hampshire, Vermont, Massachusetts, and New York State (5).

This Acadian Forest Region includes a wide variety of habitats on the hills, mountains, plateaus, and coastal plains of New England and the Maritimes, often defined by climatic differences. It is part of a "transitional forest"(6) that connects the more northerly conifer-dominated Boreal Region with the Deciduous Forest Region in the south and typically supports a mix of tree species such as red spruce, yellow birch, balsam fir, and sugar maple, supplemented by red pine, eastern white pine, eastern hemlock, and blue beech (American hornbeam).

The seaboard lowlands of the region, which include the Annapolis Valley, have a relatively mild climate, with distinctive vegetation where hardwoods play

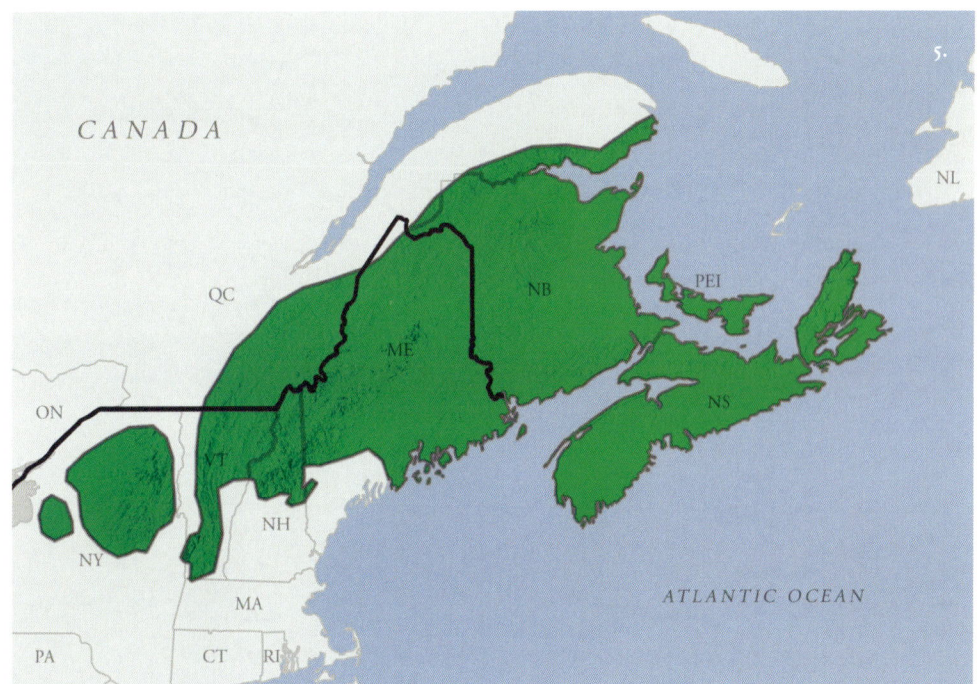

a more important role. Widespread clearances in previous centuries, and the subsequent abandonment of farms in this area, have left a mosaic of habitats influenced by local microclimates. This has resulted in a varied and interesting landscape with a wide range of habitat types and plant communities.

To show some of this rich diversity and interest, our intention was to create an approximation of the more important communities at this coastal elevation, including various types of woodlands, wetlands, coastal headlands, and residual old field meadow. We also included the sand barrens, a fragmented and at-risk dry, exposed coastal heathland in the Annapolis Valley, which is becoming increasingly rare.

To this end a great deal of research was done in the field in order to understand the nature of these habitats, the plant communities they supported, and the typical plant associations that comprised them. This was notably executed by Peter Romkey, a local woodsman and naturalist, who later went on to serve as director of the project from 2004 to 2016, and Janet Smith, one of my landscape architectural colleagues. They also put their minds to the difficulty of collecting and transplanting plant material to the gardens while preserving the plants' unique complexity and characteristics. The conclusion drawn was that the collecting of material from threatened sites needed to be comprehensive. Along with the appropriate tree canopy species in woodland, for example, we needed understorey shrubs, ground-layer plants and a healthy dose of mulch, leaf litter, rotting wood, and so on, which contained not only the important mycorrhizae on which success depended but also seeds and spores of herbs, ferns, and fungi typical of the forest floor (7). If we were collecting from bog or marshland, it was no use expecting to assemble a natural-looking collection by transplanting individual plants; we needed the whole shebang, and so we devised machinery that could lift deep bog turf, transplanting whole communities, a complete genotype, out of the path of the bulldozer and into its new home in the gardens.

I learned an early lesson from talking to Eddie Kemp, curator of the Royal Botanic Garden Edinburgh and later at Dundee University Botanic Garden in Scotland. Eddie is a pioneer in displaying plants in their natural associations, and I was struck that this approach was more informative than gardens with abstract collections. In his work, everything about the receiving site had to be right if it was going to work in the longer term: substrate, soil, pH, drainage, aspect, exposure—all had to mimic the natural conditions in which these particular plant associations thrived and remained in balance. One can never recreate precisely the natural condition in juxtaposed small and diverse areas, but getting the basics as close to nature as possible provides a good start. From there, it has been a case of constant monitoring and adjustment by the able garden staff to maintain the integrity and interest of the original design.

So, when we came to recreate the habitats in our gardens, everything was considered from the bedrock up. Calcareous woodland areas were underpinned by limestone rock and calcareous soil from quarry overburden; the Sand Barrens had sharp drainage and poor sandy soils to emulate this dry heathland type; the Bog Garden had peat over a clay liner to retain moisture, a water source dosed to achieve the necessary low pH, and measures taken to avoid nutrient ingress from surrounding areas and keep the soils poor; the Coastal Headlands area was constructed from rock and gravel on an exposed bank to provide the meanest of growing conditions typical of nature.

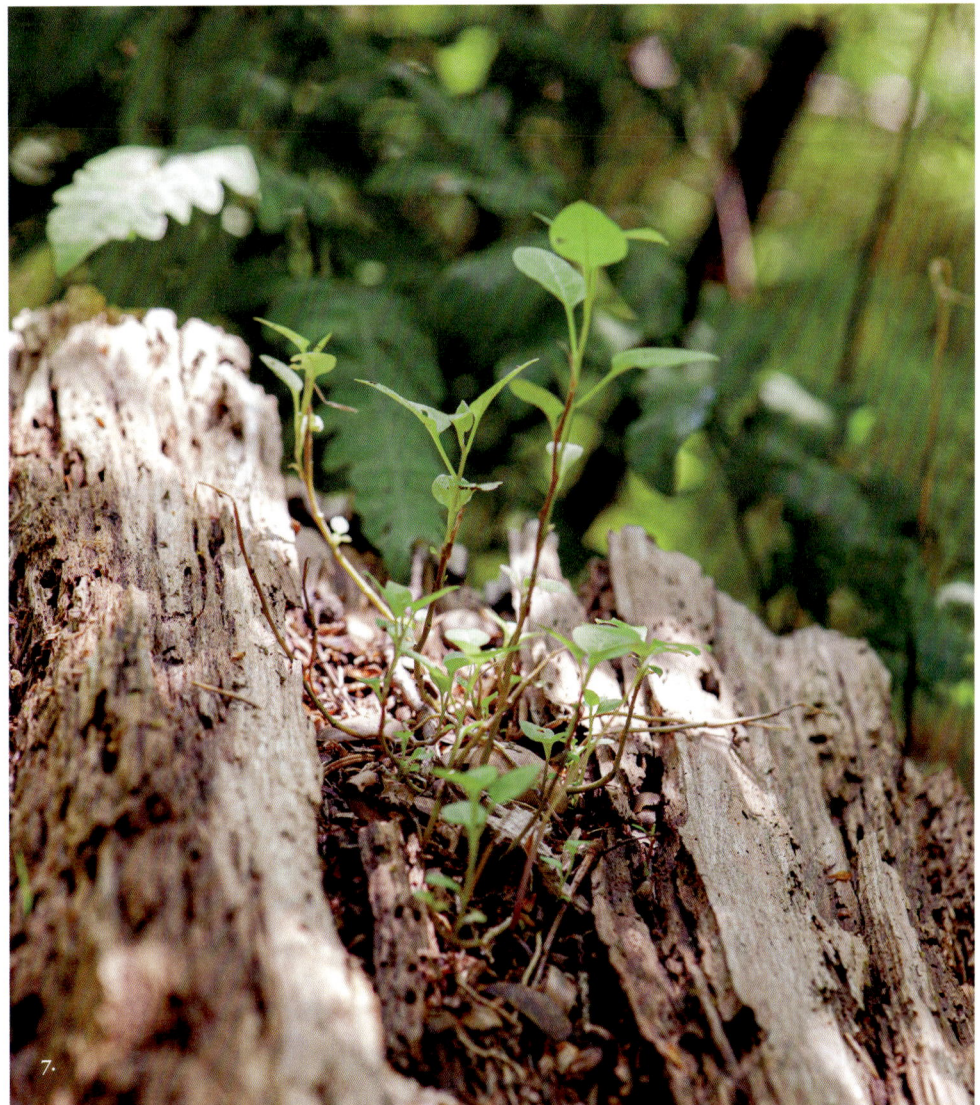

7.

## Early Research

The basis of any good project is thorough research and this one was to be no exception. Arthur Irving was keen to know where we could learn lessons from other botanical gardens, native plant displays, student commons, research facilities, glasshouses, orangeries, and of course, natural sites (8). We were not going to find another site where all these elements would be brought together. In this, his vision for Acadia University was unique. However, we would try to find the best examples of each available and, if possible, improve on them.

So it was we visited the Royal Botanic Gardens, Kew (9), those at Cambridge and Oxford Universities in England, the National Botanic Gardens of Ireland in Dublin, the Royal Botanic Garden Edinburgh in Scotland, and at the Chelsea

8. Early conceptual notes and sketches by Janet Smith.

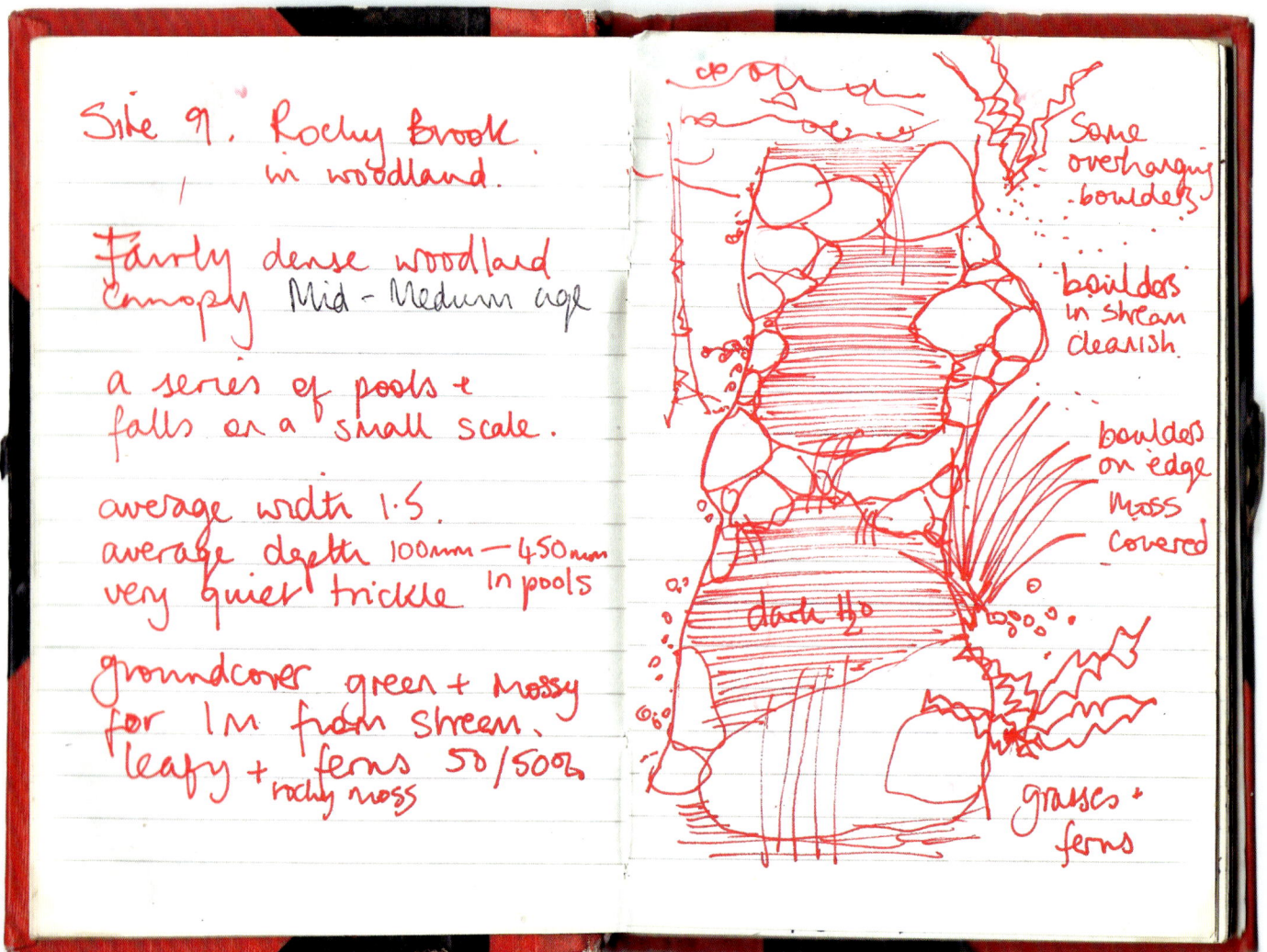

9. Waterlily House, Kew Gardens, London, UK.

Physic Garden, London, with its wonderful collection of medicinal and culinary plants. Close to the Acadian Forest Region itself, we visited two influential sites: the Garden in the Woods in Framingham, Massachusetts, where New England native plants are displayed in a garden setting with ornamental plants from a wider area, and the Memorial University of Newfoundland Botanical Garden. The latter has grown from 4 acres to an impressive 110 since its formation, showing native plants with other plants that have adapted to the climate.

We looked at the research laboratories at Duke University in Durham, North Carolina, the great glasshouses at Kew, and at the rooftop greenhouse at Harvard. We were inspired by the Classical Revival architecture at Dartmouth College and were particularly impressed with Robert A.M. Stern Architects' Spangler Campus Center, the outstanding student commons at Harvard. These visits were invaluable; we learned so much about how to develop the elements we wanted and how to combine them into a unique and special scheme.

## The Master Plan

A landscape master plan is the synthesis of many layers of constraint and opportunity on a chosen site. The plan is the solid foundation for the creative spark that lifts a site out of the ordinary. I was brought up on Ian McHarg's *Design with Nature* and fortunate enough in my early career to work with leaders in the field who saw development as a landscape- and ecology-led exercise — one where the natural attributes of the site inform the creative process, rather than something that comes purely from the designer's intellect and might as well have landed from Mars. We called it "Landscape Planning."

McHarg introduced an analytical process that enabled the many complexities of the natural and social environment to be "sieved" to a logical conclusion, but the idea is not new. In 1734, the poet Alexander Pope commanded us to "consult the genius of the place in all." This theme became known as the *genius loci*, literally the spirit of the place. Although borrowed from the Latin phrase referring to the protection conferred by the spirit being of a particular locale, it became the inspiration for the magnificent gardens at Stourhead and was adopted by the great eighteenth-century landscape architects, like Capability Brown and Humphry Repton. It came to mean that a designed landscape should first and foremost reflect the particular and distinctive atmosphere of its location. The landscape architect should work with the natural characteristics of a place, letting these special qualities inform their creation, preserving a sense of place and local distinctiveness, and giving a design a heart and soul. As Pope wrote in *An Epistle to the Right Honourable Richard Earl of Burlington* (1731):

> *Consult the genius of the place in all;*
> *That tells the waters to rise, or fall;*
> *Or helps th'ambitious hill the heav'ns to scale,*
> *Or scoops in arching theatres the vale;*
> *Calls in the country, catches opening glades,*
> *Joins willing woods, and varies shades from shades,*
> *Now breaks, or now directs, th'intending lines;*
> *Paints as you plant, and, as you work, designs.*

It is true that the special attributes of this particular site in Wolfville were not immediately obvious. It comprised a regular block of developed land on the west side of the Acadia campus, bordered by streets on all four sides. It was occupied by a variety of redundant student residence buildings, with access and terraced parking and the usual utilities, all of which would have to be cleared. Looking beyond this rather homely first impression, the site had a number of valuable assets. It had a lovely position, in clear sight of University Hall and the older classically inspired campus buildings, whose elegant brick and stone facades evoked the quiet confidence of a well-established and highly regarded seat of learning. It had interesting topography, with a marked slope from south to north, and also from east to west. It had many handsome mature trees, some of which were natives (American elm, white spruce, sugar maple), but many of which were imports (Norway maple and two handsome Chinese maidenhair trees). Best of all though, beyond the site, woodland stretched as far as the eye could see, which would be an obvious natural extension to the garden. These woods, planted by the university many decades before as a forestry exercise, were now of sufficient maturity to provide their own interest and naturalized habitats: a small stream, mixed woodland, wooded glades, and small areas of old open meadow.

The master plan would use these attributes to dramatic effect (10). As far as the K.C. Irving Environmental Science Centre was concerned, a traditional style would not only inform the architectural atmosphere of the new building but also be reflected in the symmetry and traditional design of its garden setting, particularly in the Walled Garden (11). The topography of the site was used to enhance these effects. The building on the original master plan was conceived as an L-shape, with the entrance lobby and long classical orangery (the Garden Room) facing east to the core of the campus and a wing of glasshouses facing north toward the adjacent biology building. The high brick walls of the garden defined the remaining two sides of the square. The discernible south-to-north slope permitted levelling out the formal lawns as they swept down to these enclosing walls, then breaking the slope at the building itself. Thus, the south side of the building is single storey, but the north face is a full two stories (12). Laboratories and offices are below the glasshouses, before lawns again sweep down to what is now the new biology building.

The business of constructing the master plan would be complex and multi-layered, combining the natural and the artificial, the scientific and the recreational, the wonder and the joy. Though landscape-led, it also relied on long-established design principles like enclosure, a balance of formality and informality, access and circulation, and a thoughtful palette of materials.

Botanical Gardens Support Area

Highland Park

Mixed Woodland · West Woodland

Sand Barrens

Brook · Waterfall

Coniferous Woodland

Bog

Herbaceous Bank

Quiet Lawn

Ravine

Calcareous Woodland

Marsh

Coastal Headland Display

Meadow

Deciduous Woodland

Lily Pond

Formal Lawn

Medicinal and Food Plant Garden

East Pavilion · West Pavilion

Campus Meeting Place

Walled Garden · Experimental Garden

Main Entrance

Conservatory · Research Greenhouse

Service Building

Service Yard

University Avenue

Westwood Avenue

© Novell Tullett, 1999

0'   20'   40'        80'

10. Novell Tullett Master Plan

11. Early conceptual drawing of the Walled Garden

12. North facade of the glasshouse / greenhouse and laboratory wing

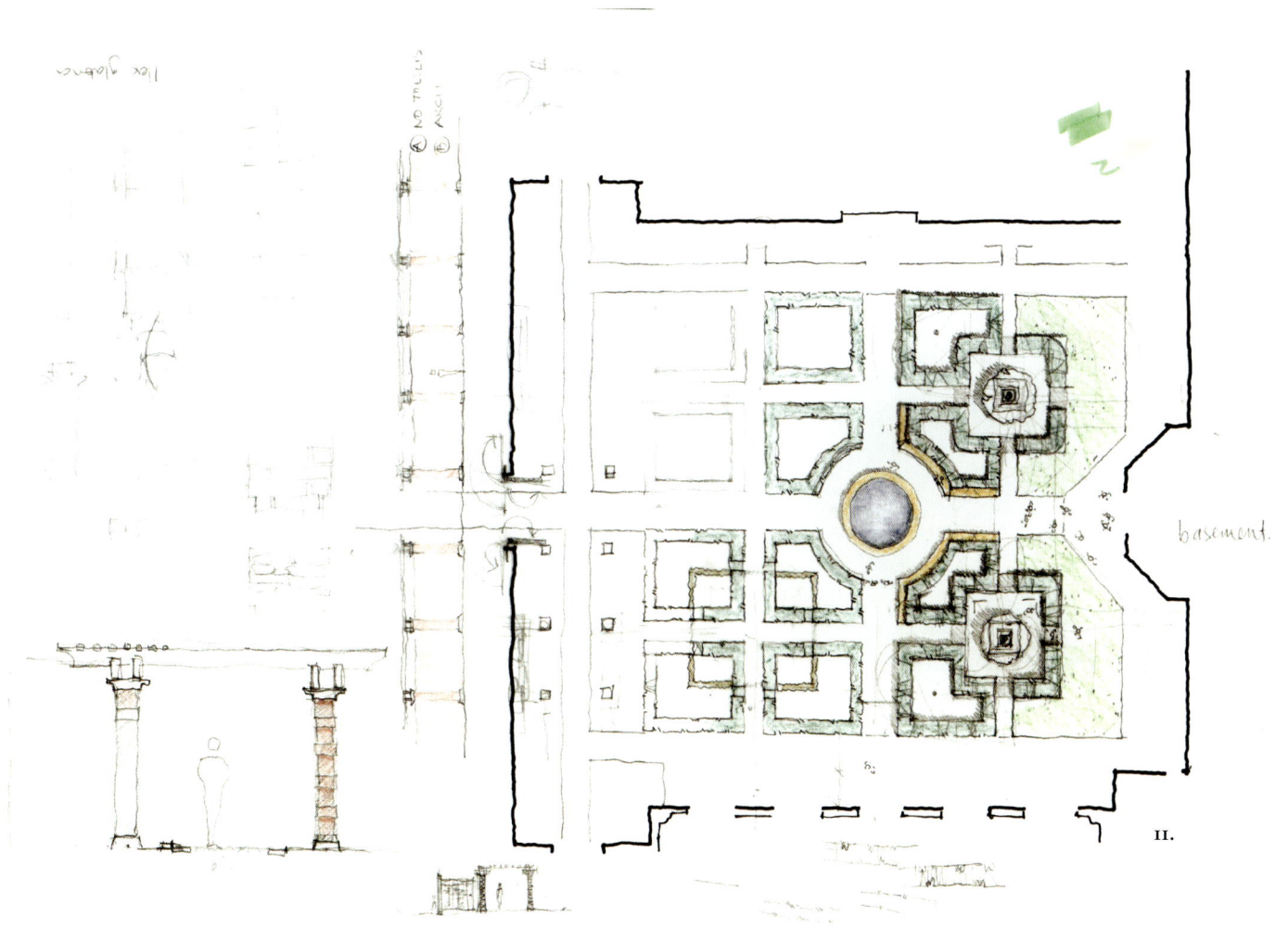

11.

12.

# Enclosure

Enclosure is fundamental to creating a distinctive space. Japanese, Chinese, Moorish, Italian, Dutch, and English gardens, indeed most of the great garden traditions, define their boundaries by enclosure, protecting the garden from the real world beyond, as a haven from the homeliness, noise, and bustle of the everyday, only allowing selected views beyond where they will add to the beauty and tranquility of the scene. In this way the experience can be controlled and directed as a piece of theatre, now hiding, now revealing a sequence of views to the viewer.

The great estates, originally owned by kings and nobles, were so vast that extraneous distractions were rarely a problem. As smaller areas of land came to be owned by those of good fortune, this developed into more of a consideration. No self-respecting owner of a country house and estate in the eighteenth century would wish, or more importantly wish his guests, to see a neighbour's land. And so this principle of visual enclosure became important. Boundaries were protected by woodland and, where this wasn't practical, by screen walls. The wooded boundaries disguised the limits of the landholding and apparent scale of the demesne, so that nothing took away from the grand design.

So it is here at Acadia. If visitors to the garden were to commune fully with nature, the illusion would be shattered if they were exposed to the day-to-day activities of a busy campus: the road traffic, student residences and domestic housing, utilities and other visual clutter of everyday living. We wanted to create *rus in urbe*, nature in the city. The various woodland types to be included here, therefore, were arranged around those boundaries unprotected by the solid enclosure created by the building and Walled Garden, to further enclose the gardens and screen out what was beyond (13). We were aided in this by retaining the existing mature trees within these areas, and by the university woodland beyond the surrounding streets, which, seen over and through our developing woods, gave the illusion that the forest was an unbroken extension of the garden (14).

13. Walled Garden with central pool and fountain

14. Woodland enclosing the oval Quiet Lawn

13.

14.

## Formality and Informality

The balance between formal and informal, maintained and natural, order and chaos, is fundamental to landscape design. If all parts are maintained to the same degree, the whole is flattened, reduced in visual stimulation and contrast. Mowing a formal lawn against wilder grass benefits both; the lawn looks even neater against its rougher cousin, the meadow and forest ever more natural against their manicured neighbour. The master plan included both formal landscape (walled garden, formal lawns, and culinary and medicinal collections) (15, 16) and more natural areas (woodland, marsh, bog, meadow, sand barrens, coastal headland, and wildflower bank) (17).

16.

17. *Sambucus racemosa*
red elderberry (top)
*Impatiens capensis*
spotted jewelweed (bottom)

## Circulation

Circulation is another key layer in the master plan, providing access and guiding the movement through the landscape to best advantage, ideally in circular eddies so that paths are not retraced to return to the start. Along the way, the careful offering of views (to hide and reveal in sequence) is a device used to add surprise and delight as the viewer is drawn along these routes, from one area of interest to the next. Long vistas punctuated by points of interest were included. One of the most compelling is from the Conservatory, on the main axis through the Walled Garden (18, 19), garden gates, and then up the great lawn to the formal lily pool fountain with the ginkgo tree punctuating the view. At this point, steps lead one up to the Old Field Meadow, where the Quiet Lawn is revealed, with its single red oak acting as a focus. From this central axis, meandering footpaths lead through the woodland areas and along the Stream, with a diversion along a boardwalk through the Bog, before recrossing the Stream and returning to the Walled Garden via the pleached Linden Walk of the medicinal and culinary collection. At every point of interest, information boards illustrate the different plant collections with examples of typical plants to spot.

In this manner, direct paths with open views of the destination give way to indirect routes, meandering, peaceful, private paths through hidden gardens and habitat. Active areas, where children can play on the lawns or concerts can take place, are not far from the sight and sound of splashing water, with stepping stones and narrow bridges to cross. These contrast with peaceful paths (20) and passive places for reflection, with occasional benches to encourage the visitor to rest and be at one with nature, or find a quiet spot to work.

The Woodlands beyond the botanical gardens site provided an ideal opportunity to extend these paths out into the wider landscape. Marked trails were cut through the woods (21), with steps and stream crossings done simply, using logs and stepping stones. Apart from the obvious delight of walking through wild woods, there were surprising features of interest here too, with rediscoveries of the original nineteenth-century Acadia farm well (22), glades, clearings rich in wildflowers (23), and a huge veteran oak along the way.

18. Bird's-eye view of the Walled Garden

20. Garden trail in the autumn

21. Woodlands trail

22. Nineteenth-century Acadia farm well along the Woodlands trail

23. *Overleaf:* Waymarker in open field

24.

25.

## Palette of Materials

The choice of materials and the details of their use and construction can make or break even the most carefully conceived and intricate master plan. In this case, it will be remembered, we were inspired by the formal yet timeless elegance of the older campus buildings, built in mellow brick, stone, and slate. So, our palette was natural building materials used in traditional ways: handmade brick, quarried stone, natural slate, bronze, iron, gravel, and timber (24).

Our classic English park benches were made from seasoned oak with mortise and tenon joints, with a bronze roundel in the seat back (25). Made by the eminent sculptor Michael Rizzello, who also designed the K.C. and Harriet Irving bronze-relief plaques in the garden pavilion, these roundels depict a crest, which he created especially for the project, with the thistle of Scotland (for the Irving family's roots), the mayflower (Harriet Irving's favourite flower and the provincial flower of Nova Scotia), and the bee, that hard-working pollinator we all rely on (26).

The walls of the traditional Walled Garden are built of the same type of brick that pave the streets of Boston, made by hand in cherrywood moulds by Messrs. Stiles and Hart. This archaic fabrication method creates brick of unusually high durability and a distinctive quality, with no two bricks exactly the same. Selecting and laying the irregular brick requires greater skill and effort than working with the standard machine-made article, and our team of master masons were able to construct walls of great character and craftsmanship. The limestone caps and copings echoed the traditional stonework in the building.

A robust sandstone was used for low seat walls (27) surrounding the beds in the Walled Garden and for the ornamental lily ponds. Designed and carved to classically inspired profiles, the ponds and fountains echo the building style and help to define the character of the more formal area. They are also a great hit with children in hot weather.

So hard to resist in municipal jurisdictions, concrete or asphalt surfaces would have detracted from the ambience of the building, thus natural stone paths and terraces were used around the building and in the Walled Garden, reinforcing the formal nature of these spaces. Paths into the gardens were constructed of naturally cementitious limestone "hoggin," a type of all-in aggregate limestone favoured in the royal parks and gardens of London and relatively easy to maintain. These give way to narrow trails through the woods, constructed with

**26.** A bronze medallion of the Centre's crest is set into every wooden bench.

28.

a light limestone base, but not surfaced, allowing a gradual accumulation of leaf litter, moss, and ground-layer plants to colonize and cover, while still offering a measure of firmness and drainage. A handsome wrought-iron fence surrounds the perimeter of the larger garden, a refined counterpoint to the colour and texture of the nature alongside (28).

In every way, the garden construction materials were chosen to complement and harmonize with those of the building, so that the one would be seen as a seamless part of the other.

1, Grand Pré, in the Annapolis Valley

# An Exceptional Balance of Form and Substance

## JOHN LEROUX

The Annapolis Valley is one of Canada's most storied meeting places of architecture and landscape (1). It has sheltered European settlers for over four hundred years, and for many thousands before by the Mi'kmaq who lived off the bountiful bay and soil. A symbiotic rapport between humans and the coastal terrain is a deep-seated ethos that goes to the very heart of this area. At its centre is the historic town of Wolfville and the adjacent Grand Pré, a UNESCO World Heritage Site, both in a region known by the Mi'kmaq as Mtaban ("mud-catfish catching ground"). Grand Pré is an emotional heart of Acadie for transformative reasons, and Wolfville is a beautiful, affecting community, especially for the thousands of Acadia University alumni around the world who spent foundational years living and learning in the town.

So much of the Wolfville/Grand Pré/Mtaban story is of connecting building and nature: from the sustainable Indigenous structures and settlements of the pre-contact era, to the sophisticated Acadian aboiteaux dykes that converted tidal flats into rich farming fields, to the ordered orchards that made the valley the apple basket of Canada and the United Kingdom, to the current thriving of wineries and vineyards. This remarkable legacy has no better contemporary example than the K.C. Irving Environmental Science Centre and Harriet Irving Botanical Gardens at Acadia University (2). Celebrating nearly twenty years of serving the students and staff of Acadia, the Irving Centre and Gardens were conscious gifts to the world—open and welcoming to everyone. It holds widespread attraction for scientists, gardeners, historians, architects, landscape architects, prospective students and their parents, and the simply curious.

Combining facilities for scientific research and instruction with meeting and gathering spaces, the Irving Centre and Gardens encourages members of the university and wider community to connect with nature and the natural sciences. The elegant building looks to the restrained classicism of the university's older structures yet has state-of-the-art research and display greenhouses, laboratories, and well-equipped teaching rooms. With its interior centred on generous social spaces, the Centre's wings enclose a carefully crafted Walled Garden outside, with natural gardens and woods beyond.

2. Main entrance to the K.C. Irving Environmental Science Centre and Harriet Irving Botanical Gardens

The K.C. Irving Environmental Science Centre and Harriet Irving Botanical Gardens are a brilliant achievement, attaining that rarest of feats where an altered landscape is made whole again by the careful addition of sensitive architecture and design. The story of their conception, planning, and execution is a noteworthy instance of a discerning client, patron, architect, and landscape architect working together with a common vision and shared values. The project has tangibly changed Acadia University. It has also changed individuals, whether through recurring visits or in solitary flashes of insight or inspiration: from a eureka moment in the light-filled greenhouse, a quiet moment in the Garden Room, or running one's hand along the spiral stair's polished wood handrail.

This is the building's story.

## The Acadia Landscape

Acadia University is considered one of Eastern Canada's most attractive campuses. Its roots go back to an 1838 founding with two faculty and twenty-one students. From there, the university grew modestly for much of the nineteenth century. Situated on a gently sloping hill running up from Main Street, the campus offers little evidence of the institution's early architecture, as fire and change constantly shifted the built landscape. Dominating Acadia's venerable hill today, the central university building, University Hall (3), with its tall clock tower and Corinthian portico, is the third one on its site. Both nineteenth-century predecessors were gutted by fire.

The lower Acadia campus is charming and harmonious, although its architecture is a diverse mix of styles that span a century and a half. Older structures such as the Second Empire–style wood-framed Acadia Seminary (1878) (4), the red-brick Georgian Revival Carnegie Hall (1909), the eclectic Palladian-styled Emmerson Hall (1914) (5), the rough-stone Horton Hall residence (1915), and the late Beaux Arts classicism of University Hall (1925) all make for a wildly varied family, but they do get along. Across the street behind a curtain of ivy is the late Greek Revival War Memorial Gymnasium (1921), handsome and refined beside its later chunky modern additions. Farther up the hill, Fountain Commons (formerly McConnell Hall, 1926), War Memorial House (1945), and Chipman House (1960) were cautious Georgian designs — the Manning Memorial Chapel (1963) being somewhat more ornate — but these would have a deep effect on the future appearance of Acadia. They established Georgian as a go-to architectural style, and red brick as the exterior material of choice.

3. University Hall (1925), with its tall clock tower and Corinthian portico

Like most campuses, a modernist construction wave met the baby boom during the 1960s and 1970s. It paused the Georgian aesthetic, although red brick held on where it could. The exposed concrete Brutalist style was used for the New Acadia Students' Union Building and Huggins Science Hall, and the unadorned modern forms of Acadia's Beveridge Arts Centre, Divinity College, and Crowell Tower speak of both the design restraint and economic limits that were affecting campuses across the country in the 1970s and 1980s. Periodic new buildings and renovations would later take place, with the most significant at the turn of the century; its roots set by an old friend of the university.

In 1996, Acadia president Kelvin Ogilvie asked Canadian industrialist Arthur Irving if he would consider taking on the role of university chancellor. A proud Acadia alumnus, Irving's collegiate roots extend even further back to his father, K.C. Irving, who attended Acadia in the late 1910s. Arthur said, "I will do it if I can do something for the students," so the project started as a reflection of Irving and his wife, Sandra, wanting to add something of consequence to Acadia. Half a decade later, they would be cutting the ribbon for a facility whose impact would reach far beyond this particular spot in Nova Scotia.

## Emerging Vision

The concept of the Centre and Gardens evolved from early conversations between Arthur Irving, Sandra Irving, Kelvin Ogilvie, and Alex Novell. Ogilvie notes that "the big ideas originated from Mr. and Mrs. Irving. I had the privilege of working with them to flesh some of it out, but the key ideas of the environmental science centre and gardens came from them." Alex Novell was brought in at the onset to help focus on the vision of what would best serve Acadia University and dovetail with the local environment. An esteemed landscape architect and partner of Novell Tullett of Bristol, United Kingdom, Novell had developed a strong working relationship with the Irving family through his involvement on significant landscape design projects in Saint John and Bouctouche, New

4. Acadia Seminary (1878)

5. Emmerson Hall (1913)

Brunswick. There was no better professional to help guide an emerging endeavour that was landscape-led.

The group initially discussed improvements to Patterson Hall (the university biology building) (6), such as an improved glass entrance or greenhouse addition, as the then greenhouse was in disrepair. This relatively modest idea of glass concepts was well received, but the Irvings were clearly thinking bigger than this. In the summer of 1997, Arthur Irving and Alex Novell walked through an underused residential area above Patterson Hall on University Avenue. It was situated on a prominent Acadia street directly across from the older campus core and within clear view of University Hall, but it also connected to acres of mature woods on the southern edge of the university. The substantial site was ultimately chosen. Arthur Irving bought the houses running up to Highland Park (now Park Street), some were moved, and the preparation and planning began.

Novell recalls: "Arthur asked me if I would come up with a concept for a garden which would celebrate the wild flora of the Maritimes, but also include a meeting place for students. We talked about extending the garden into the woods beyond." The connection was perfect as both of Arthur's parents were passionate about nature. His mother, Harriet, had a love of flowers, and his father, K.C., as anyone in the Maritimes knows, was deeply interested in trees.

Arthur Irving is also enamoured of trees and gardens, and these were envisaged in what the Centre and Gardens could be. The idea of creating a meeting place for friends was one of Arthur's earliest thoughts, inspired by his own student days. As Arthur and Sandra Irving thought about the opportunities for student engagement,

6.  Patterson Hall (1929)

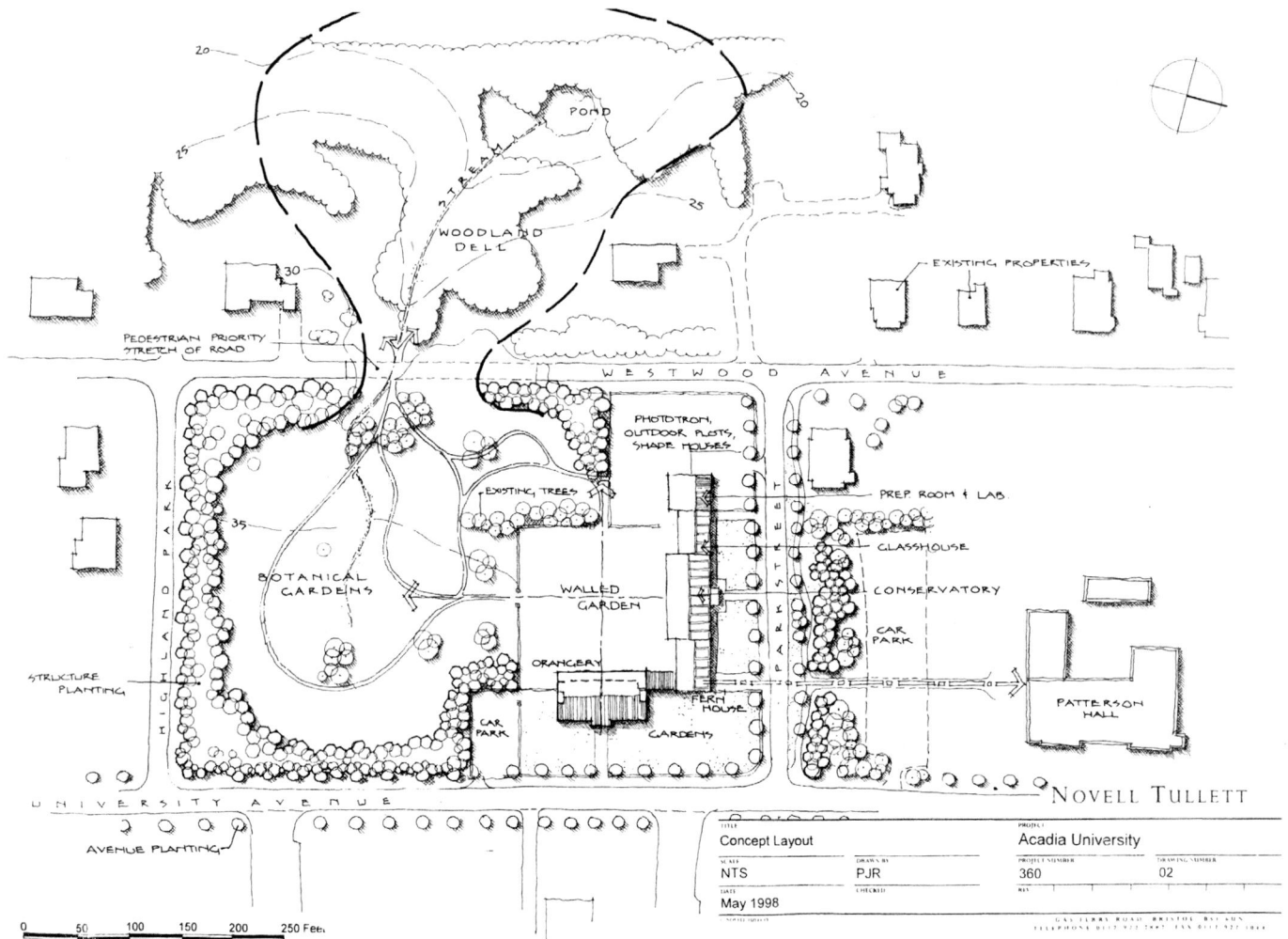

The figure contains the following labels: STREAM, POND, WOODLAND DELL, EXISTING PROPERTIES, PEDESTRIAN PRIORITY STRETCH OF ROAD, WESTWOOD AVENUE, PHOTOTRON, OUTDOOR PLOTS, SHADE HOUSES, EXISTING TREES, PREP. ROOM & LAB, GLASSHOUSE, CONSERVATORY, BOTANICAL GARDENS, WALLED GARDEN, CAR PARK, STRUCTURE PLANTING, ORANGERY, CAR PARK, FERN HOUSE, GARDENS, PATTERSON HALL, AVENUE PLANTING, UNIVERSITY AVENUE, NOVELL TULLETT

| Concept Layout | | Acadia University | |
|---|---|---|---|
| SCALE NTS | DRAWN BY PJR | PROJECT NUMBER 360 | DRAWING NUMBER 02 |
| DATE May 1998 | CHECKED | REV | |

0   50   100   150   200   250 Feet

7. First detailed sketch concept by Novell Tullett (1998)

undegraduate scientific research opportunities, scholarship, and mentorship at Acadia University, these values all became integral parts in the development of the Centre.

During their consideration of glasshouses and conservatories, Ogilvie recalls talking with Arthur Irving "about what a glass enclosure can mean to a circumstance. There's nothing nicer in the spring or winter [than] going into a greenhouse, the sun coming through, sitting in the warmth.... Instinctively, we knew we wanted a place for people, and the plants would provide an ambience for it." The Irvings and the project team began looking at renowned glasshouses in Great Britain and the United States, from February 1998 through to the summer of 1999. This started with a visit to Cambridge and Oxford, where Novell set up a meeting with botanist John Parker, director of the Cambridge University Botanic Garden. Parker's early advice was critical, as were the team's further greenhouse visits. These quickly became appropriate as many are found on university campuses, particularly in the United States, such as those operated at Harvard, Duke University, Dartmouth College, Smith College, and many others.

Bounded by three critical aspects — site, students, and service — the Irvings and Novell envisaged an integral architectural-landscape target that would satisfy their ambitious goals. A proper building had to enrich the planned botanic garden that would feature plants, trees, and vegetation from the Acadian Forest Region. Novell ascertained that such an architectural outcome should be set close to the garden entrance for administration and research; it had to have a glazed greenhouse or conservatory; outbuildings for horticultural staff and equipment; and for the public it needed a light-filled "orangery" room, visitors' shop, and café. The first detailed sketch concept by Novell Tullett in May 1998 was surprisingly in tune with what we see today: an L-shaped building at the northeast corner of the site, surrounding two sides of a formal English walled garden (7). This led to botanical gardens extending out southward and pathways meandering farther to the existing mature woods. Novell's shorter building wing that paralleled University Avenue held the orangery (intended as a student meeting place), while the longer east-west arm contained a research greenhouse, conservatory, and lab facilities. The Walled Garden was axially connected to both the Orangery and the Conservatory. It was classical British planning that spoke of order, elegance, and a humanist tradition.

With the conceptual scheme and early research in hand, the next step to find the right architect was critical. Fortunately for everyone involved, one of the most renowned in the profession was ultimately selected.

## Stern Concepts

To choose an architect, the Irvings and Ogilvie visited a number of American campuses and spoke to a half-dozen established architecture firms. In the end, Robert A.M. Stern Architects (RAMSA) of New York City was selected. The firm was appointed jointly with Novell Tullett to design the building and gardens as an indivisible entity. As a sign of faith and as an indication of how important he considered the job, Robert Stern committed to take full responsibility and personally oversee every detail of the building. It was a rare pledge as the RAMSA firm would typically have dozens of complex architecture jobs on the boards at any time.

Stern called the K.C. Irving Environmental Science Centre and Harriet Irving Botanical Gardens "a very important project in the context of my evolution as an architect." It was one of the first major university buildings RAMSA had designed, and it helped lead the firm to become one of the most trusted college architects in North America. One cannot discuss the K.C. Irving Environmental Science Centre and Harriet Irving Botanical Gardens without laying out RAMSA's vast array of achievements and built works. They have helped distinguish the firm for excellence in design and client satisfaction over decades.

A graduate of Yale's architecture program in 1965, Stern worked for the internationally renowned American architect Richard Meier for several years. In 1969, he formed the firm of Stern & Hagmann with a fellow student from his days at Yale, and in 1977, he founded the successor firm RAMSA. For many years Stern concurrently taught architecture at Columbia University and until 2016 was dean of the Yale School of Architecture.

RAMSA has designed projects for the Walt Disney Company and landmarks for Harvard, Yale, and many other universities. RAMSA designed the Comcast Center in Philadelphia, the George W. Bush Presidential Center in Dallas (8), the headquarters of Mexx International (9), Pauli Murray College and Benjamin Franklin College at Yale University (10), the planning and refurbishing of New York's Times Square, and campus master plans for such institutions as Georgetown University. Stern himself hosted an architectural television series for PBS and has written a number of important books on historical and contemporary architecture.

Stern's work has been widely published and exhibited. It is in the permanent collections of the Museum of Modern Art, the Metropolitan Museum of Art, the Deutsches Architekturmuseum, and the Art Institute of Chicago. In 1976, 1980, and 1996 respectively, he was among the architects selected to represent the United States at the Venice Biennale of Architecture. Robert A.M. Stern is a critical figure in twentieth-century architecture, and having him design a project at Acadia University was an exceptional opportunity.

The Irvings were determined that the aesthetics and function of the Acadia building had to complement the excellence of the projected academic program and research facilities. Key to this objective would be assembling the best team possible. No building of this scale is ever designed by a single individual, and in forming a design team, Stern appointed two trusted associates: Graham Wyatt and Preston Gumberich. The RAMSA team concentrated intensely on the potential of the site as they further refined the initial Novell Tullett conception of the building. They considered it essential and liberating to square out the entire block, allowing a full landscape precinct instead of an irregularly shaped property. Taking a thoughtful and informed approach to the new building, exhaustive study and walks throughout Acadia provided much of the impetus. Wyatt recalls connecting with the selected site right away:

> The site is very important. As you walk out through the portico of
> University Hall and look up to your right, there was a hole that was
> missing. There were some houses up there. We were standing on the

8. George W. Bush Presidential Center, Dallas

9. Mexx International headquarters, Voorschoten, Netherlands

10. Pauli Murray College & Benjamin Franklin College, Yale University

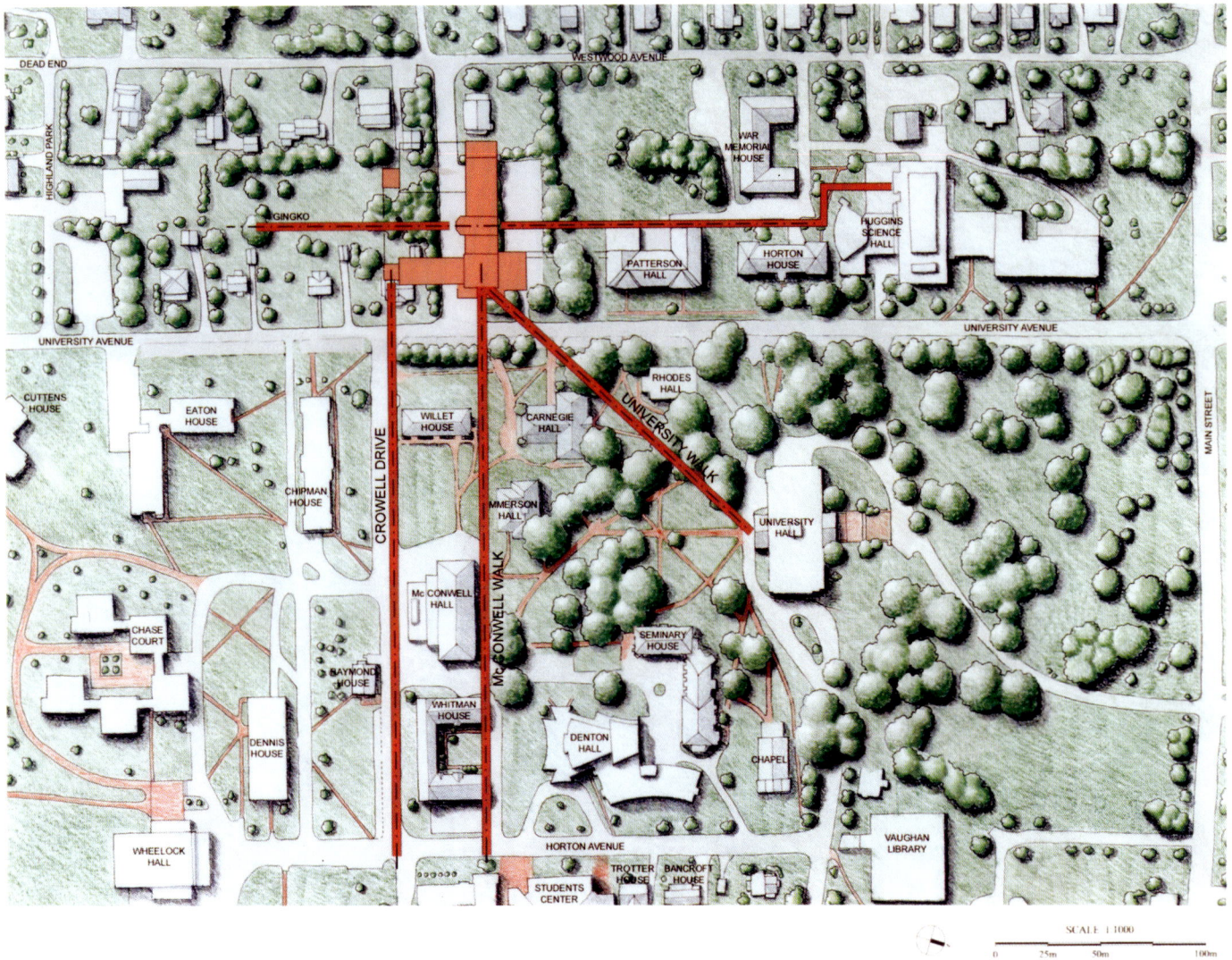

11. RAMSA study drawing showing the importance of site axes

south-facing portico of University Hall looking back. It was very clear early on that there should be something that occupied that space rather than it being vacant.

Tapping into the potential of the empty site becoming a central hub and destination required consideration of what was needed to "complete" the lower campus. What did the new site want to be? Did it want to be a corner? Did it want to be a pivot? Did it want to be a gate? In the end, it wanted to be all of those things. RAMSA thought of this project from the beginning not simply as a building and a garden but as an act of campus-making. Wyatt hoped it would be "a new thing in its own right, but also an addition to a campus. We wanted to affect the greatest positive change we could to the campus through the placement of the building and the garden" (11).

Given the organic garden/forest aspect of the project, it was critical that the architectural design bring a sense of order, but not constraint. The building and its spaces had to work, but they also had to be inviting. This came from a respectful appreciation that every part was of equal importance, both interior and exterior. The interconnectedness of working space to social space to intimate space was essential, as was the graceful flow from inside to outside, and once outside, from formal to wild—into the Acadian forest. There was tremendous poetic potential in traversing layers from built to wild. The architects wanted there to be no single clear threshold that you would cross. Somehow you could pass seamlessly from one to the other and just be "in nature" without realizing where you made the transition.

Thinking first of the building, then a procession of greenhouse, walled measured garden, outside open garden, and finally woods, there was a strong design sense of the garden transitioning from the formal to the less formal to the truly natural. Surroundings would get more and more wild, layers becoming progressively unconstrained until they're liberated. This concept was worked out at length with RAMSA and Alex Novell. They wanted it to feel like you were able to walk out of the Conservatory and into the wilderness. Stern wanted to meaningfully separate the students rushing to their lab class from students choosing to "dream in the lounge." Fostering a place where students could dream gave the Novell Tullett orangery idea its full due.

An orangery was a large room or dedicated wing of fashionable European manors from the seventeenth to the nineteenth centuries. Frequently used for entertaining, orangeries would often contain fountains, grottos, or other decorative "follies," as staging was part of the social experience. They were early versions of greenhouses where exotic plants, orange trees, and fruit trees were protected during the winter, hence the name. By the eighteenth century, orangeries were seen as a "must have" feature in European country house gardens. They were the prominent form of conservatories until the mid-nineteenth century, when large-scale cast-iron frames and plate-glass sheets became available. This allowed the modern architectural marvel of Joseph Paxton's famed London Crystal Palace to see the light in 1851.

The Irvings and the design team visited two noted orangeries in London, which became key precedents for the K.C. Irving building's scale, design, and effect. Attributed to Nicholas Hawksmoor, the Kensington Gardens' orangery (1704-05) is a long brick pavilion whose symmetrical form is belied by its ornate Baroque design and details (12). Its recurring march of tall multi-paned windows and arched brick ends with their recesses and quoins make for a façade that revels in being at once calculated and playful. This was a building for pleasure. The Kensington example likely had a strong effect on the design direction of

12. Kensington Gardens orangery, London (1704–05)

13. Kew Gardens orangery, London (1761)

14, 15. An early clay model and elevation study of the ornamental style that was an early consideration for the complex.

56

the final Acadia scheme. A kindred connection emerges in comparing the Irving building main façade's three sections from right to left (prominent ornate entry with columns, Garden Room with tall repeating windows, and arched garden pavilion) to the Hawksmoor building from the centre to the left (prominent ornate entry with pilasters, orangery room wing with tall repeating windows, and arched projecting end).

The other London orangery that made an impact was at Kew Gardens (13). The white stone building was designed in 1761 by Sir William Chambers. Somewhat more restrained and ordered in its Georgian appearance than Hawksmoor's earlier precedent, its middle run of five arched windows is reflected in the side walls of Acadia's Garden Room.

Initial RAMSA sketch ideas are fascinating aspects of the genesis of the final product. Casting the net wide, a number of early elevations and clay models showed a hyper-ornamental style of Hawksmoor-like British Mannerism with a main entry section and side wings (14, 15). Maritime restraint soon came into play, and a more simplified Palladian approach was taken. RAMSA's first concepts explored a "three-bar scheme" where an E-shaped plan of three heavily

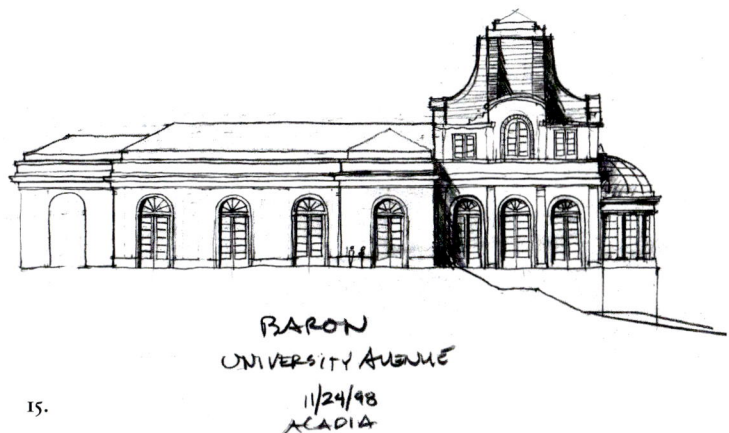

BARON
UNIVERSITY AVENUE
11/24/98
ACADIA

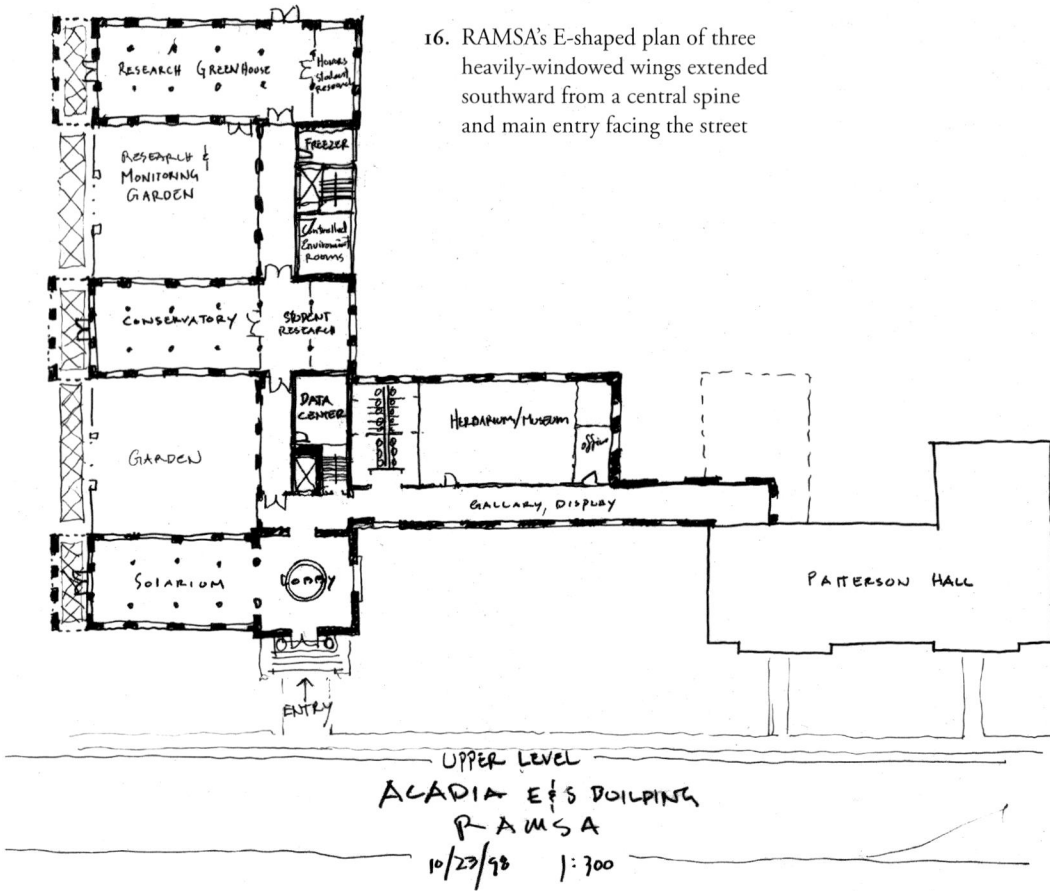

**16.** RAMSA's E-shaped plan of three heavily-windowed wings extended southward from a central spine and main entry facing the street

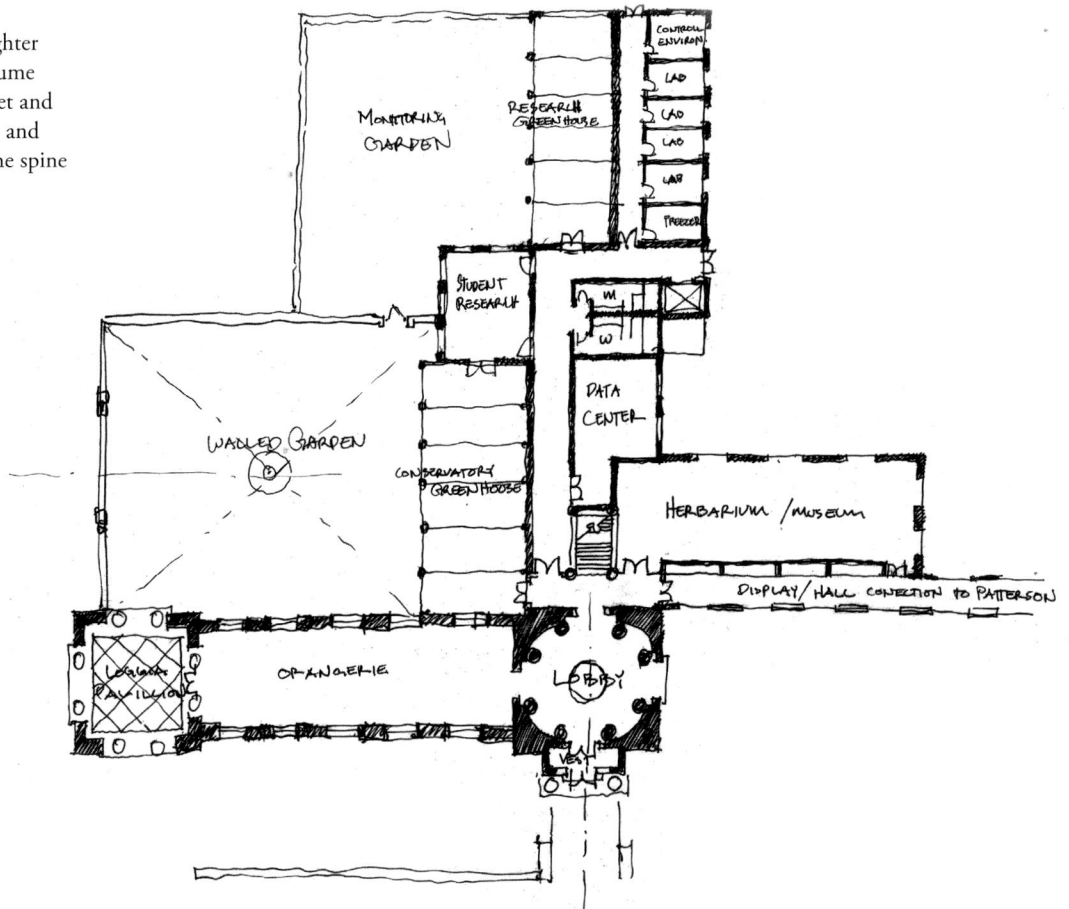

**17.** "Bar Scheme" brought a tighter form and a more linear volume running back from the street and entry, with a large solarium and greenhouse at the core of the spine

18.

19.

18. Architect's model of the
    "L scheme"

19. Ohrstrom Library at
    St. Paul's School in Concord,
    New Hampshire, 1991

windowed wings extended southward from a central spine and main entry facing the street (16). U-shaped plans were also considered. A series of further concepts simply labelled as "bar scheme" brought a tighter form that held a more linear volume running back from the street and entry, with a large solarium and greenhouse at the core of the spine (17). This eventually transformed into the preferred option the architects called the "L scheme," which was similar to the earlier Novell Tullett sketch proposal (18). It combined the tall, more decorated and formal entry pavilion as the entry focus, with a public orangery space running parallel with the street, and the greenhouse and labs running perpendicular, back from the entry. This enabled the eventual walled courtyard garden to enjoy a south-facing protected microclimate.

Architects often expand on their past schemes for their latest projects, and RAMSA was no exception. The firm's 1991 Ohrstrom Library at St. Paul's School in Concord, New Hampshire, is one of their most celebrated buildings and a fitting formal precedent (19). The same design team of Stern, Wyatt, and Gumberich who quarterbacked the Acadia project designed Ohrstrom, and the trio would be in charge of many of RAMSA's growing academic building commissions. Although the earlier library's appearance is a response to its Gothic campus, and the Acadia project affirms its Georgian roots, they both share a tall right-hand asymmetrical entry, with a longer side wing of repeating full-height windows. Both the Ohrstrom Library and the Irving Centre have a cross axis at the entry end in their respective plans — like a church where the crossing happens. Stern calls it a "head and tail" idea.

Through the design and construction document phases, meticulous testing was fully embraced. No detail was too small. Two mock-up walls of varying exterior bricks and stone bases were built in front of the nearby Carnegie Hall. They were observed through a full set of four seasons to gauge how they looked and performed. Another instance involved Arthur Irving riding high above the tree canopy in the bucket of a boom truck. He wanted to see first-hand the exact location and view from the proposed second-storey patio off the boardroom. This was to ensure a seamless vista over the water to the iconic cliffs of Cape Blomidon and also a more subtle view (and an equally important one) looking back onto campus.

Construction began in the fall of 1999, a century after the birth of Arthur Irving's father, K.C. Irving. Once initiated, it was easy to see that the building's scale fit perfectly with the rest of Acadia (20). Through the success of this project, RAMSA and Novell Tullett were given the task of doing a full Acadia campus plan, which was unveiled and adopted by the board of governors in 2002.

20. K.C. Irving Environmental Science Centre under construction, August, 2001

## Final Design

The K.C. Irving Environmental Science Centre and Harriet Irving Botanical Gardens officially opened on September 14, 2002 (21). With formal ceremony on the front entry patio, Arthur Irving passed the building keys to President Ogilvie. At the event podium, Arthur emphasized, "This gift is the realization of our vision to create a special place in memory of our parents. My father would have been especially pleased that the K.C. Irving Environmental Science Centre is a place where students, academics, and members of the community come together."

Other speakers that day included Robert A.M. Stern, Alex Novell, Hans Klohn (the project manager and long-time Irving construction project adviser), and Ogilvie, who called the facility a "place of enormous beauty, tranquility, and repose." The 65,000 square-foot building and six-acre gardens were poised to begin their mission, fully equipped and furnished with state-of-the-art laboratory gear and beautifully crafted furniture and fittings.

The red-brick building with Indiana limestone trim, wood windows, slate roof, hand-pressed brick (no two pieces alike), and metal-framed glasshouse were carefully crafted at the turn of the twenty-first century, but the building's Georgian architectural language would be familiar to someone living two hundred years ago. The traditional form and style of the edifice were celebrated by Stern, who described it as "among the best buildings that we've ever done." Appreciating campuses that have coherent structures, Stern says architects who hurl comments about his traditionalism are missing the point. They question why he does not always advocate modern building designs, as is largely done by the profession today. Stern is, in fact, an expert at contemporary design where he sees fit. Look no further than his Mexx headquarters in the Netherlands, Greenspun Hall at the University of Nevada in Las Vegas, and his initial Valley Forge scheme for the Museum of the American Revolution.

In the case of the Acadia project, he avowed that the search of novel forms for novelty's sake would be a dead end: "We're not doing a modern building because by the time we finished, it would already look dated and have nothing to do with the campus." This aligns with his credence that architecture must have a humanist approach at its core, connecting with culture as a whole and helping "repair the threads" of the local landscape. As Stern decisively articulates, "We prepare for the future by drawing upon the past." Without gimmicks or flashy strategies, the traditional emphasis and details of the design allow the clarity of the building to speak effectively and effortlessly.

21. Artist's watercolour rendering of the final design

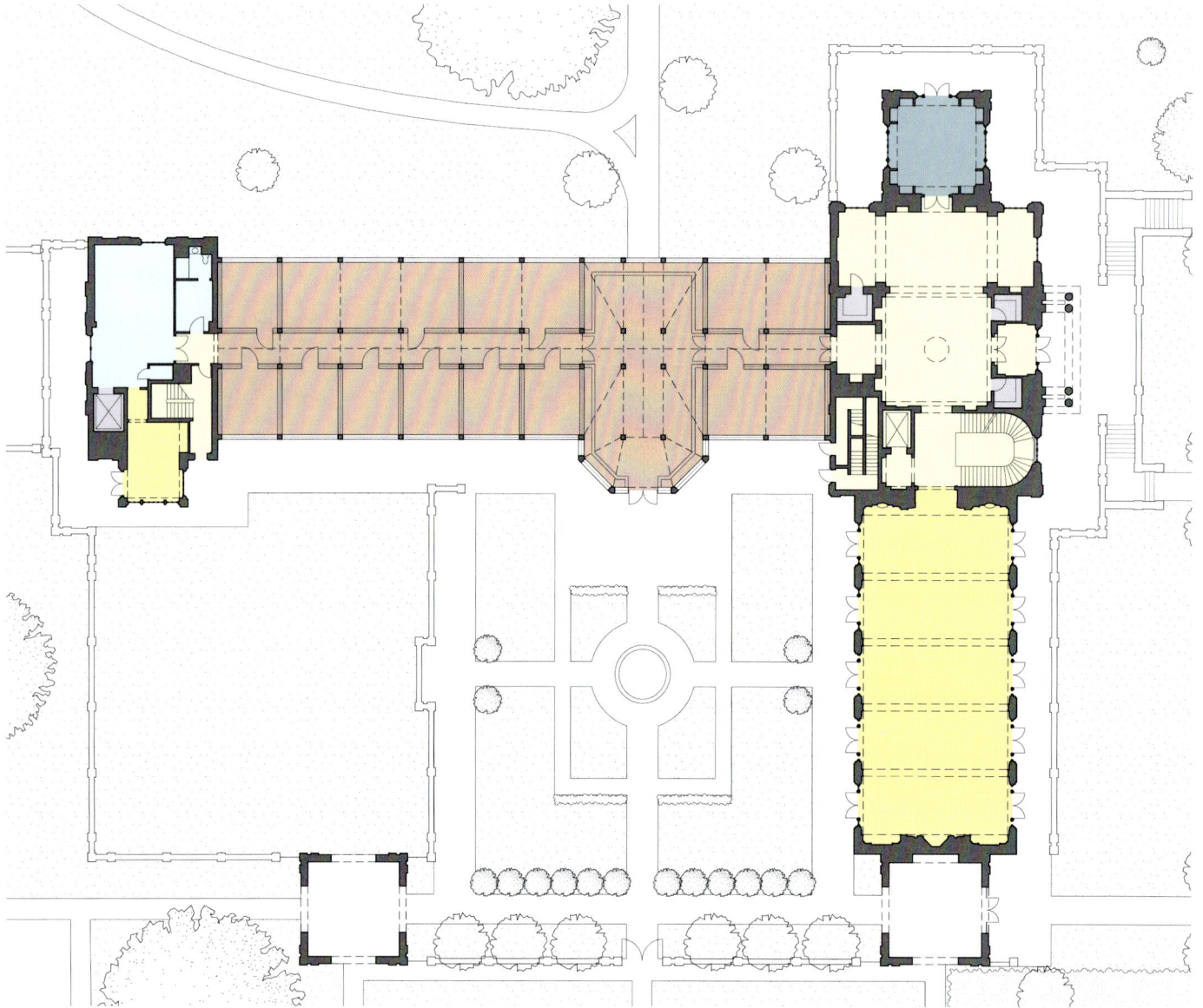

GROUND FLOOR PLAN

| | CIRCULATION | | LABORATORY | | CONFERENCE |
|---|---|---|---|---|---|
| | LOUNGE | | LAB SUPPORT | | OFFICE |
| | LIBRARY | | GREENHOUSE | | SERVICE |
| | CLASSROOM | | | | |

# K.C. IRVING ENVIRONMENTAL SCIENCE CENTRE
## ACADIA UNIVERSITY
### WOLFVILLE, NOVA SCOTIA, CANADA

N

0    8    16         32 FT

SECOND FLOOR PLAN                                                23.

LOWER LEVEL PLAN                              24.

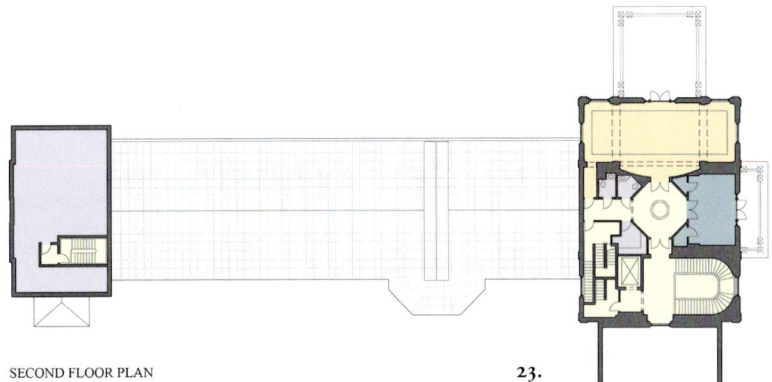

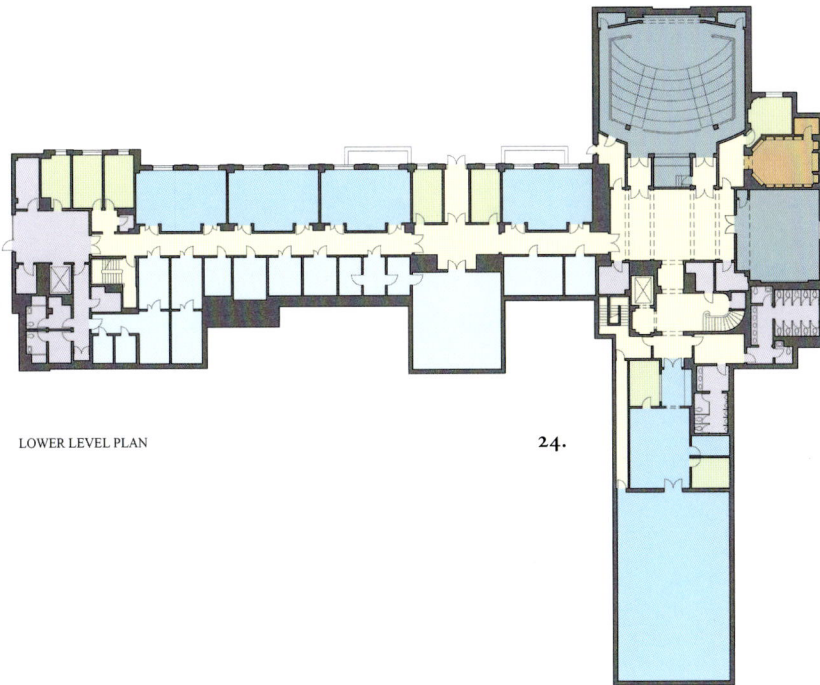

The Irving building uses an L-shaped plan, with the entry and larger public spaces running along a north-south axis beside the street, while the greenhouse/laboratory wing extends east-west back into the site (22–24). Classical architecture benefits from visual rules developed over millennia, and this clear rationale bodes well for the sloping site. The multi-layered corner section anchors the building. Its hip-roofed volumes are set back as they reach upward, cresting at a large cupola with a bellcast roof (25). Lightening the mass and visual weight of the front façade are the single-storey wings that almost pierce through the building centre. These two sides connect with the run of arched windows but differ with their stone ornament and roofs. The outside treatment and volume of the downhill meeting room matches the corner garden pavilion at the opposite end of the front façade (26). Both extensions sport the same stone entablature and paired pilasters, although one's arch is filled with a pleasing fanlight window, double door, and sidelights, while the other is an open gateway to the garden. The latter's archway curve bounds gilded wrought-iron lettering announcing that you are entering the "Harriet Irving Botanical Gardens" (27).

Approaching the main entry, the craftsmanship of the building is striking (28). Carved stone pillars and wrought-iron railings enclosing the stone steps and terrace hint at the details inside. Etched into the portico face is an inscribed "K.C. Irving" in Roman letters, while aside the door is the "1999" cornerstone. The building's temple-like entry porch with its Tuscan stone columns gives the

25.

25. The multi-layered corner section anchors the building. Its hip-roofed volumes are set back as they reach upward, cresting at a large cupola with a bellcast roof.

26. Garden pavillion at the the southeast corner

27. Arched entry of the garden pavillion with cast-iron gate

26.

K·C·IRVING

29.

30.

28. Main entrance portico

29. U-shaped spiral staircase

30. Hand-crafted bench at the entrance vestibule.

31. *Overleaf:* In the lobby, the oculus opens to the upper floor and is aligned to the cupola above.

building material gravitas, but it also makes a convincing statement: prepare for something special as you pass through these doors. As current Acadia president Peter Ricketts says, "The building is inviting you in."

The orientation and layout are clear and apparent upon entering the lobby, as two main pathways cross in front of you under an oculus above. These powerful axes are carefully designed, bringing order as soon as you arrive. Once past the Irving Centre's entry portico you walk toward the lab wing but are instantly struck by the bright light and décor of the Garden Room immediately to the left.

The U-shaped spiral staircase between the entry and the Garden Room is a joy to walk up, with blue slate treads and a wrought-iron railing capped with a stained wood handrail (29). The quality and refinement of the woodwork are immediately felt once inside the Centre. Meticulously handcrafted wood trim, panels, benches (30), and carved flourishes abound, all made in Moncton, New Brunswick, as Arthur Irving proudly notes. In fact, from the Acadia job, that same Moncton firm secured a furniture contract from Harvard. Stern recalls, "We chose materials that we thought would have enduring value and that people would relate to. The woodwork inside is incredible. I don't think we've ever done any better woodwork than in that building."

Standing directly under the oculus open to the upper floor and roof cupola (31), to the right is a café and social area with a meeting room and outside deck beyond (33); straight ahead is the greenhouse with its public spaces and labs (32); and to the left is the gorgeous Garden Room with its inviting warm yellow walls, arched coffered ceiling, and pendant light fixtures (34). The Garden Room feels majestic and grand, but not overwhelming. The walls are a yellow Venetian plaster, done with a *strié* technique of faux painting where brushed glazes create a soft, subtly striped texture. The colour was to be warm so that even in the winter it would feel welcoming and comfortable. The Garden Room is the light-filled social heart of the Centre with the wood-burning Rumford fireplace, custom-built wood and leather furniture, and classically ornamented walls with raised pilasters and a row of five large arched windows on both sides of the room, allowing sunlight at all times of the day.

32. Exterior view of greenhouses and lab wing

33. Meeting room off the entry lobby

34. Garden Room

35.

36.

Essential to the space is the Steinway grand piano. The Irvings, Peter Romkey, and several faculty members from Acadia's School of Music chose it in person directly from the Steinway factory in New York. Beyond the perpetual social and study use, the room has hosted weddings, concerts, and important meetings. Brydone Charlton, a 2016 Acadia music grad, called the building "a refuge to all students at Acadia," and one that had particular significance to music students. The Garden Room was regularly used as a performance venue by faculty, students, and visiting artists. Charlton recalls, "Our professors would perform improvised music with an ever-changing lineup of faculty once a week in the Garden Room. The students, inspired by the professors, started a similar group. The space was very important to our experience at Acadia."

35. Upper level boardroom

36. Teaching auditorium

37. The herbarium houses more than 140,000 botanical specimens.

The building's upper level features a meeting room above the entry porch, washrooms, and a long boardroom and outside patio deck overlooking the bay beyond, the space democratically serving as much for students and classes as for "official" board business (35). The lower level offers a 124-seat teaching auditorium with great acoustics and finishes (36). It quickly became one of the most popular teaching spaces on campus. Biotechnology labs are situated under the greenhouse, and the E.C. Smith Herbarium is under the Garden Room. The Herbarium is possibly the oldest plant collection in the region and certainly one of the most extensive with over 140,000 specimens (37). Arthur Irving was adamant in ensuring proper facilities for this scientific showpiece. The Centre has space for more than a century's capacity for growth of samples, set within a state-of-the-art rolling mobile filing system they had seen at the Missouri Botanical Garden Herbarium in St. Louis, Missouri.

The main-level greenhouse spaces are a hit to the senses as you arrive through the lobby double doors. The counterpoint to the brick/stone/wood of the main building is powerful as the greenhouse almost dematerializes with its latticework of glass panels and whitewashed steel frames (38). You are encouraged to stop and linger at the main Conservatory, where a large moss-covered granite boulder and its pleasant fountain are surrounded with the greenery of ferns and local plants (39). Farther ahead are the open lab spaces, usually filled with students busy managing their experiments (40). These research labs are cutting edge.

38.

39.

40.

38.  Exterior view of the Conservatory

39, 40. Inside the Conservatory and Greenhouse labs

41.

42. Gates from the Walled Garden lead from the Conservatory into deep nature.

The atmosphere in each research glasshouse can be carefully controlled, with the levels of oxygen and carbon dioxide specifically regulated. The high-tech nature of the labs and conservatory lobby (41) also runs through the rest of the building. The Georgian aesthetic can be deceiving at times, where specialized systems include such efficient features as groundwater cooling from the aquifer below the site.

The stronger pull, however, is to the left at the Conservatory, where you find yourself at the beginning of one of the most compelling features of the complex — where the Environmental Science Centre and the Botanical Gardens fuse together along the central path, connecting the building to deep nature. The traditional construction materials of the Centre once again become apparent when you step from the building into the Walled Garden: hand-pressed brick; the wrought-iron gate (42); carefully crafted wooden benches (43) with bronze medallion inserts by British sculptor and coin designer Michael Rizzello; the Hampstead granite water table along the base of the building (44); and a circular sandstone water pool and fountain. Novell Tullett designed the Walled Garden in its entirety, including the surrounding brick walls, stone bench-walls, fountain, and gates. The entrance gate, elegantly titled with "Harriet Irving Botanical Gardens," was fabricated in Salisbury, England, by master metalsmiths. The stone used in the garden and fountains is "Dorchester stone" from the old Beaumont

Quarry near Memramcook, New Brunswick—the same quarry that supplied stone for the boundary walls of Central Park in New York City.

The pair of garden pavilions at the southern corners is among the most calculated design aspects of the whole site, but also one of the most delightful (45). Inspired by the corner pavilions at the Royal Naval Hospital and Queen's House in Greenwich Park, London (46), these decorative, anchoring elements form a gateway to the formal botanical garden. With their openness and permeability, they also make a fitting margin for the dematerializing of the architecture as it edges onto the garden and woods. Gumberich recalls, "In a more pragmatic sense, we knew that there was going to be an entrance to the garden that wasn't necessarily going to have to go through the building all the time, if it happened to be closed. So that was the driving force." Satisfying a larger urban design role in the campus, the eastern pavilion gracefully completes the visual axis that runs fully through the campus via Crowell Drive.

**43.** Wooden benches with bronze medallion inserts

**44.** Grey Hampstead granite water table along the base of the building

45.

46.

45. South face of the K.C. Irving
    Environmental Science Centre
    showing the pair of garden pavilions

46. Naval Hospital and Queen's House
    in Greenwich Park, London

47. Large glass globe lights with copper
    strapping hang from the pavilions'
    coffered ceilings

Large glass globe lights with copper strapping hang from the pavilions' coffered ceilings (47). Known as "armillary spheres," these were ancient models
consisting of a spherical framework of rings, centred on the Earth or Sun, representing lines of celestial longitude, latitude, and other astronomical features.
While their lineage and symbolism are most likely overlooked by many who pass
under them, these quiet details speak to science, geometry, history, and the desire
for knowledge.

Looking back after two decades, Sandra Irving measures the building's success
by how quickly and how widely it was embraced by the student body of Acadia.
It has also been a surprise in how the Centre and its rooms have shaped a reflective and tranquil mood:

## 47

I love the Garden Room, and seeing students there when we enter. It always reminds me of Arthur's first thought about what he wanted the building to be: about students. It was meant to be a social place with conversation and maybe background music, but instead it's become a quiet place. We never envisaged that. It took on an identity of its own. My favourite space is near there, before you enter the working greenhouses. It is a beautiful spot with a large rock we chose from Hampstead, New Brunswick, and brought here. It's a special place because it has this piece from home, the tranquility of running water, and the warmth of familiar plants and greenery.

Ogilvie echoes this view. On the quiet space versus the dynamic, he asserts, "The quiet nature of it during the academic year is the highest reflection of value to the university community. It's not silence like in the old library concept. Students at each table are often having a dialogue, they're working on projects, and so on. It's comfortable. You can do that in that room because of the way it's designed."

Ray Ivany, Acadia University president from 2009 to 2017, understood the tremendous value of the building and its spaces, allowing it to speak openly to future students:

Often, I'd be meeting in my office with a prospective student and their family, and they've been visiting some of the best universities across the country. You can see on their faces that they're listening to me, but they're thinking, "I'm sure [Acadia is] a great university, but it's a university not unlike others that we're considering."

I remember the first day I did this, and I've done it dozens and dozens of times since. I said, "Let's take a walk around campus. I think it's palpable that you will be able to feel what this institution does is different." As part of that, I took them to the K.C. Irving Environmental Science Centre. We entered the building and we weren't even in the Garden Room yet, but were walking toward it. They looked at me and said, "Now we get it." It happened time after time, after time, after time.

In 2007, Vincent Scully, one of the most respected architecture critics in modern history, declared the architectural achievement of the Acadia project to be more than considerable:

> It may be that Stern's most memorable intervention in a campus is the environmental science building of Acadia University in Nova Scotia. It builds up blocky Georgian masses, densely squeezed and high shouldered, and the more dramatic because rising off a steeply sloping hill.... But it also seems utterly Canadian, tough and strictly contained against the cold.... The whole complex is a powerhouse in every way, perhaps Stern's masterpiece so far, classically aggrandizing its Georgian campus.

There is no question that the K.C. Irving Environmental Science Centre and Harriet Irving Botanical Gardens have physically and metaphorically changed the landscape of Acadia University. The dignity and shared aspirations for students and the wider community are embodied in not only the program of the Centre but also in the architecture. It is a rare accomplishment when human inspiration and social benefit are the undisputed drivers of a building endeavour—not tight budgets, economies of scale, or compromise by committee. In return, the respect shown to the facility by students, faculty, and citizens who visit is profound.

The K.C. Irving Environmental Science Centre and Harriet Irving Botanical Gardens also changed the landscape of university architecture in Eastern Canada.

48. A circular sandstone water pool and fountain in the centre piece of the Walled Garden.

The 1970s, 1980s, and 1990s were not good decades for campus architecture in the Maritimes. The Acadia project came at an opportune time of re-evaluating physical character in our universities. It showed beyond a doubt that such an exemplary accomplishment can be done here and that quality buildings can have a measurable effect on university life and attracting new students. Did the Irving Centre break the dam? Very likely, attested by the recent wave of excellent new institutional structures in the Maritimes. Ogilvie observes, "It's fair to say that a great number of universities — not just in Atlantic Canada — when they're planning something new, have visited here. To see how this facility sits on the campus, and how it reflects. People think now in a broader way about how a facility impacts the campus."

The Irving Centre is considered one of his most privileged achievements during his tenure as president of Acadia, and Ogilvie is delighted that "this place has had an impact on every person who has come to Acadia, and every person who has gone through this facility. People have changed because of their experience in the Centre." Romkey, the facility's former director, considers it the social heart of the Acadia campus. He affirms, "This is a place that students could depend on. It was always open. We never shut down, not one day. Three hundred and sixty-five days a year, we're open every single day, and during study periods we stay open all night." Romkey recalls that during the infamous "White Juan" hurricane-strength nor'easter of February 2004 that shut down Nova Scotia for days and widely knocked power out, he ran the entire Centre on generators. It was the only place on campus that had heat and power. Around three hundred students were sleeping in the Centre, effectively making it a shelter and refuge, where it justly existed for the safety and comfort of students.

Graham Wyatt credits much of the success of the Centre and Gardens to Arthur Irving, his values, his altruism, and his confidence in the expert team he helped assemble: "Arthur is a very discerning client, and a great advocate in making sure that we were able to do the right thing. The standard is set high, and that's not always easy. It means that you've got someone there who is willing to work with you to achieve it."

It may seem paradoxical for such a beautiful and stirring endeavour, but at its core the K.C. Irving Environmental Science Centre and Harriet Irving Botanical Gardens are about humility. The building and gardens are not about a patron; they are about the students and about connecting to the community. The project is a testament to the power of nurturing the greater good and of honouring time. It is not only built for today's students but also for those who will come to Acadia University a century from now. It is a place that embraces tangible contact with nature, with the Acadian Forest Region, and with one of the finest works of collegiate architecture in Canada. It is a place that looks to the past to affect the future. As a centre of excellence, of learning, of understanding nature and the environment, it is more than just a building in a garden. It has become where we gather to understand our place on the Earth.

1.  Mature *Acer saccharum*
    sugar maple

# The Making of the Gardens

ALEX NOVELL

## Existing Trees

The existing trees were a key asset throughout the Harriet Irving Botanical Gardens (1). They provided shelter and shade and a framework for the garden design and lent a character that reflected the mature parkland setting of the old campus so beloved by students. The best trees were identified and their root zones marked out for protection as buildings were removed, foundations and utilities excavated, and contours reshaped to create the new garden topography. Non-native trees like Norway maples and a big European copper beech, although theoretically *personae non gratae* in a native plant garden, were nonetheless helpful in achieving the overall aesthetic and so have been retained, at least until the new planting matures. Once the newly planted native trees are sufficiently mature, they can selectively be removed in the future.

Retaining the two existing *Ginkgo biloba*, the maidenhair tree from China, was a difficult sell to the more purist members of faculty, but the trees are on the axis of the building, one to the north, and one to the south (2). In a layout that relies on classical symmetry, at least in the immediate setting to the building, to have removed these as non-native and undesirable would have left two important vistas empty of focus. They were kept. Apart from their obvious visual appeal in this case, *ginkgo* trees are of great interest to the biologist, being neither conifer nor broadleaf and representing some of the earliest trees to have developed on the planet. Only one species, *Ginkgo biloba*, remains of this ancient genus of angiosperms.

2. One of the two existing *Ginkgo biloba* trees whose position reflect the classical symmetry of the site plan.

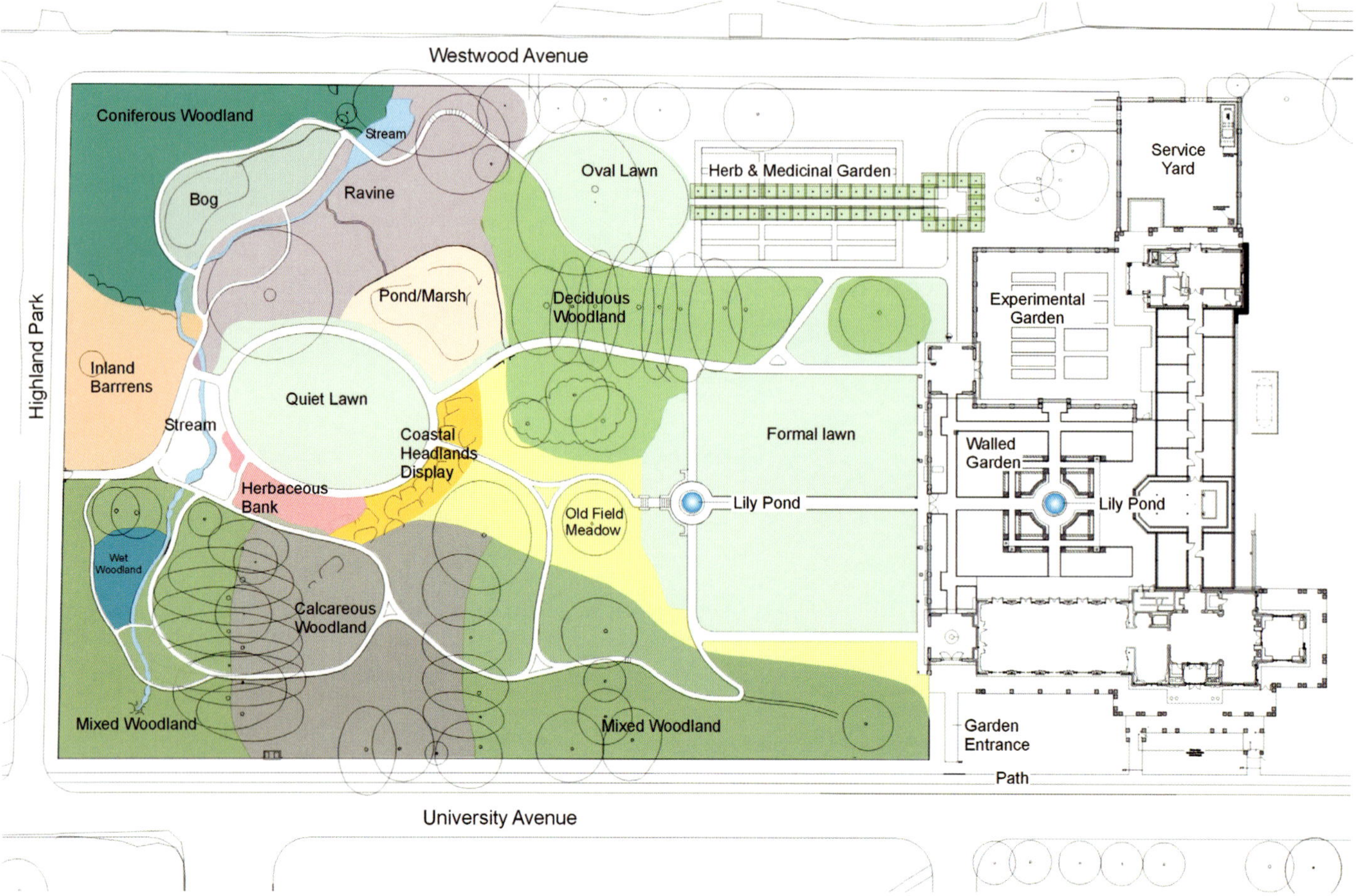

Westwood Avenue
Coniferous Woodland
Stream
Bog
Ravine
Oval Lawn
Herb & Medicinal Garden
Service Yard
Pond/Marsh
Deciduous Woodland
Experimental Garden
Highland Park
Inland Barrrens
Quiet Lawn
Stream
Coastal Headlands Display
Formal lawn
Walled Garden
Herbaceous Bank
Old Field Meadow
Lily Pond
Lily Pond
Wet Woodland
Calcareous Woodland
Mixed Woodland
Mixed Woodland
Garden Entrance
Path
University Avenue


## Topography and Surface Water

Once the building location and grades were set, this established the framework for the remaining garden design (3). The east-west slope offered an opportunity in the southern, more remote part of the site not to be missed. There was no natural water, a key component of a garden, on the site we inherited, though the woodland beyond did have a brook. The considerable grade difference made for interesting changes in level and provided the ideal topography for our own faux naturalistic stream (4), which, with the ornamental lily ponds (5) and the pond at the marsh (6), provided the movement, sparkle, and reflective qualities of water that we wanted. Our stream ran from multiple piped "springs" in the southeast corner of the site following its southern edge, tumbling over a rocky waterfall midway (7), and slowing as it passed the Bog Garden on its path to a collecting pond, from whence it was piped back to its source.

A bentonite clay liner extended well beyond the stony stream bed, providing marshy habitat along the route. The rocks for the waterfall were excavated carefully and reassembled in exactly the same natural formation on-site. It was painstaking work, but the end result looked natural, as if the stream were always a part of this landscape. One of the nicest compliments paid, but also rather frustrating, was from someone who visited the garden for the first time and told us, "You have put in some lovely trails. We really enjoyed walking through the woods and learnt a lot from all the information boards." They had no idea that the whole thing was created from scratch by clearing a fairly recent building site.

3. Framework for the garden design showing the various habitat zones

4. Wooden bridge over the stream

5. Circular lily pond at the edge of the Formal Lawn

6. Pond at the Marsh

7. *Overleaf:* Waterfall and stream

4.

5.

6.

## Soils and Drainage

The basis of any planting design is the soil. Agricultural topsoil was no good to us. High levels of nitrogen, which leaches rapidly out of the soil, and phosphorous and potassium, which don't, quickly become unbalanced without more input. Elevated levels of these artificial fertilizers encourage "lazy plants," plants that are very poor at taking up nutrients and pile in where they are freely available. These common ruderal "weed" species, which in the wild are limited to small areas, would quickly take over and dominate their more refined and delicate cousins. The high quantities of the seeds of these undesirable plants in agricultural soils, which can survive for many years, would be a constant headache.

*Pteridium aquilinum*
bracken fern

In nature, the opposite is true. Wild plants have adapted to living in their own particular niche. They are often extremely good at taking up nutrients under natural conditions, meaning that they can survive in surprising variety and abundance in the poorest soils and harshest locations. Natural systems rely on the carbon cycle: the constant recycling of organic material by bacteria, earthworms, fungal mycorrhizae, birds, large and small mammals, a host of insects, and insect larvae. Not only are all these organisms necessary to sustain a balance of plant life in a wide variety of soils and conditions (acid, neutral, alkaline, clay, loam, sand, wet, arid, impervious, free-draining, and everything in between), but also many wild plants have adapted to, or come to rely on, particular organisms for their nutrients.

Take the oak, for example. Healthy oaks, living with the mycorrhizae that sustain them, can live many centuries. When their root zones are exposed to plowing and artificial fertilizers, which disturb these important fungi, they become stag-headed and decline much sooner. It is not the effect on their own roots but on the organisms on which they rely. Orchids, too, will not grow without their particular symbiotic mycorrhizal association, and plowing pasture will wipe them out. Interestingly, when returned to permanent grazing, the orchids will begin to recolonize from the soil seed bank after a few years, as the soil mycorrhizae re-establish. This wide range of natural conditions and symbiotic relationships, and the ability of plants to adapt, gives rise to the great

variety of native flora in the region. If we were going to emulate this in our garden, we would need a similar approach.

So we built our own natural soils from the rock up. Where, for example, we wanted Calcareous Woodland, we built the limestone rock bed in an area with the right drainage. To this we added overburden from limestone quarrying, and then a healthy dose of litter from the floor of native calcareous woodland, ensuring that we imported the conditions necessary for the biological activity present in that habitat. We didn't just plant trees, but with Peter Romkey's help, brought in whole mats of vegetation: trees, seedlings, understorey shrubs, ground-layer plants, ferns, fungi, soil, and leaf litter.

This process was done with each of the woodland types. Deadwood was brought in too, and left to decompose (9), providing a home for countless organisms and giving the trees the nutrient boost they would expect in the wild (10). The larger logs were even placed in the same orientation as they were found, to ensure that mosses and lichens would have a new microclimate as close as possible to the original. The results have been impressive, and twenty years on, we have what resembles natural woodlands, with the soils and plant associations typical of a particular woodland type.

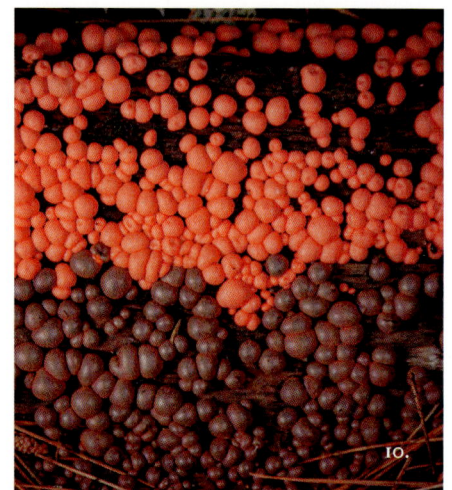

The Bog (8), located beside the Stream, needed waterlogged, nutrient-poor, acidic peat soils. We built a contained basin with a commercial bentonite clay liner, the material they use for sealing waste pits and preventing toxic leaching. Deep turfs were cut from a bog under threat from peat extraction, with a specially designed excavating bucket, ensuring that we not only had the complex plant communities intact but also the acidic organic soils that supported them. A supply of water, independent of the Stream, which could have been too nutrient-rich, was dosed to the right pH to maintain the necessary wetness and acidity. A cut-off drain round the perimeter was intended to ensure that we did not have nutrients from the surrounding areas migrating into the Bog.

The Bog required a constant supply of water to replenish that lost to plant uptake and evaporation, but the Freshwater Inland Marsh needed a more seasonal flow. By operating simple sluices diverting water from the stream (11), we could control the water height, creating spring "freshet" conditions but allowing the marsh to dry out in summer, as in nature.

By varying the shape of the land, we vary runoff, aspect, and exposure; variance of substrate, soils, and surface litter provides a range of pH, nutrient, and drainage characteristics; surface water management allows a range of wet or dry conditions; and the retention of existing trees provides immediate shelter and shade. Building on what the site offered, we were able to create the full range of habitat types we sought to emulate.

8. Bog Garden plants

9. Felled and dead trees provide valuable compost to the forest floor.

10. *Lycogala epidenstrum* wolf milk's slime

11. Simple stone and wood sluices divert water from the stream to the Freshwater Inland Marsh.

# Habitat Types and the Choice of Plants

ALEX NOVELL and
MELANIE PRIESNITZ

A great deal of research was done to identify typical plant associations within the main habitat types of the Acadian Forest Region. In such a wide geographical area and complex mosaic of plant communities, there is inevitably overlap. Some plants are more adaptable and can thrive in a range of habitats; others are more specialized and confined to particular locations. In selecting plants to celebrate this diversity in relatively small garden areas, we needed to concentrate on key indicator species and plant associations in each to draw out the distinctions between them. Many of these plants mentioned can be found in the appendix, arranged alphabetically by their botanical name.

## The Conservatory

A large central glasshouse stands as a focus on the central axis of the Walled Garden (1, 2). A "false winter" can be achieved by lowering the temperature to a comfortable five degrees centigrade, just sufficient for vernalization of the diverse collection of native plants. As light levels rise in the spring, the temperature can be increased gradually to promote flowering and leaf-break in deciduous species, while snow still covers frozen ground outside. However, this subterfuge is not good for the plants in the long term, and the collections are changed every few years to give them a full cold dormancy period outdoors.

An impressive granite boulder, draped in rock polypody ferns (*Polypodium virginianum*), was brought from Hampstead, New Brunswick, and placed before the building was erected. Water trickles from a concealed feed over the moss-covered face of the rock into a small reflecting pool below, fringed with further rock polypodys, Christmas fern (*Polystichum acrostichoides*), and evergreen wood fern (*Dryopteris intermedia*). These are all evergreens, able to photosynthesize throughout the year, storing sugar-like compounds in their leaves that act as antifreeze.

1. Looking towards the garden from inside the Conservatory

2. Walled Garden and
   Conservatory

3. Seating space in the Conservatory

Large terracotta pots, hand-thrown and signed by Italian master potter Mario Mariani, contain large bayberry plants (*Morella pensylvanica*), which have deep-green leaves, catkins in spring, and light-blue waxy berries (3). Other species in the collection include showy native perennials, such as swamp milkweed (*Asclepias incarnata*), the scarlet cardinal flower (*Lobelia cardinalis*), and blue vervain (*Verbena hastata*), a plant of shores and marshes that can reach 1.5 metres in height.

## The Experimental Garden

Twelve self-contained beds lie outside the research greenhouses, sheltered by a walled enclosure. Many experiments have been done here over the years. As a notable example, research was recently done into eastern mountain avens (*Geum peckii*), a globally at-risk plant found in only two locations on Earth, both within the Acadian Forest Region. Faculty, staff, and students at Acadia have been working with the Mersey Tobeatic Research Institute in Nova Scotia to learn more about its growth characteristics, factors affecting transplanting success, possible mycorrhizal associations, and the restoration potential through a field study on Brier Island, Nova Scotia.

Other experiments have included investigating the use of native willows (*Salix* spp.) for remediating hydrocarbon spills; a study of the critically endangered sand-barren plant frostweed (*Crocanthemum canadense*); and long-term study of how growing media affects plant health and fruiting in highbush blueberry (*Vaccinium corymbosum*).

## The Walled Garden

The Walled Garden is part of the setting of the K.C. Irving Environmental Science Centre. Sheltered and contained by eight-feet-high brick walls, it echoes the walled gardens of country houses. These were usually brick-faced to retain the warmth of the sun and used to produce vegetables, fruit, and flowers for the house. They were often associated with glasshouses and orangeries, where plants would be propagated and tender specimens kept over winter. In our case, it is a recreational space, an outdoor room where faculty, students, and visitors alike can relax, work, and hold alfresco meetings. It is formally laid out, to complement the style of the building, with bluestone and gravel walks, a central fountain, oak benches, and low seat walls in sandstone (4).

The planting is entirely native to the Acadian Forest Region. The walls are clothed in Virginia creeper (*Parthenocissus quinquefolia*), giving stunning fall colour (5). Clipped hedges subdivide the space and form a backdrop against which flowering plants are displayed; taller hedges are composed of bayberry (*Morella pensylvanica*) and lower ones of inkberry (*Ilex glabra*). Highbush blueberry (*Vaccinium corymbosum*) (6) has been used to fill the parterre around the fountain, bright green when it first comes into leaf, through darker green, bronze, and ultimately a vibrant fall scarlet. Spring and summer flowering shrubs like the tall, arching serviceberry (*Amelanchier canadensis*), bush-honeysuckle (*Diervilla*

**4, 5** *Overleaf:* Fall colour in the Walled Garden

6.

7.

8.

6. *Vaccinium corymbosum*
   highbush blueberry

7. *Rosa virginiana*
   Virginia rose

8. *Symphyotrichum novi-belgii*
   New York aster

9. East gate into the Walled Garden

*lonicera*), and wild Virginia rose (*Rosa virginiana*) (7) attract pollinating insects to the garden and have attractive berries in the summer and fall. Perennials such as mounds of bluets (*Houstonia caerulea*), the spikes of red bells of the cardinal flower (*Lobelia cardinalis*), and the pretty trailing mayflower (*Epigaea repens*) — the floral emblem of the Harriet Irving Botanical Gardens — offer a variety of form and colour. With high-summer flowering asters like the heart-leaved aster (*Symphyotrichum cordifolium*) and New York aster (*Symphyotrichum novi-belgii*) (8) providing masses of light-blue daisies, there is interest in the garden throughout the year (9).

The remainder of the botanical gardens covers some six acres, and includes the Formal Lawn, the Quiet Lawn, the Woodlands, the Stream, the Bog Garden, the Freshwater Inland Marsh, the Old Field Meadow, the Sand Barrens, the Herbaceous Bank, the Coastal Headlands, and the Medicinal and Food Plant Garden.

## The Woodlands

Woodland is the natural climax community. It provides a rich and varied layered habitat of tree canopy (10), understorey shrubs, young trees, a ground layer of flowering plants, mosses and liverworts, and fungi and ferns among rotting stumps and logs. Variation arises in the transition between the Boreal coniferous forest to the north and the largely deciduous woodland to the south. We find stands of mainly conifers, where acid soils and shady conditions lead to minimal understorey and relatively low biodiversity; predominantly deciduous woodland with more neutral soils, higher light levels in early summer, and greater biodiversity (11); and mixed woodland, with both conifer and hardwood species. There are also interesting specialist habitats like calcareous woodland found on naturally occurring gypsum and limestone outcrops and wet woodland, widespread where there are poorly drained areas.

In the Coniferous Woodland, typical species include eastern hemlock (*Tsuga canadensis*), the tamarack or larch (*Larix laricina*), white pine (*Pinus strobus*), red spruce (*Picea rubens*) (12), and balsam fir (*Abies balsamea*). Lichens such as varied rag lichen (*Platismatia glauca*) cover the trunks and branches. Much of the forest floor is dark, supporting only mosses, fungi (14), liverworts, and the unusual ghost flower (*Monotropa uniflora*), a parasitic plant without chlorophyll that feeds on soil mycorrhizae and often appears only after rain (15). In clearings and woodland edges, we find orchids, like pink lady's-slipper (*Cypripedium acaule*), the provincial flower of Prince Edward Island, together with goldthread (*Coptis trifolia*), starflower (*Trientalis borealis*), mayflower (*Epigaea repens*), Nova Scotia's provincial flower, and the exquisite painted trillium (*Trillium undulatum*) (16).

Throughout the Deciduous Woodland, broadleaf species provide a canopy only in summer and early fall, allowing sunlight to penetrate in other seasons. Tree species include the sugar maple (*Acer saccharum*), the yellow birch (*Betula alleghaniensis*) (13), once widely used to skin birch-bark canoes, and the American beech (*Fagus grandifolia*), together creating spectacular fall colour. Understorey shrubs thrive in the higher light conditions and include beaked hazelnut (*Corylus cornuta*) and fly-honeysuckle (*Lonicera canadensis*), which provide food

11.

12.

13. *Betula alleghaniensis*
    yellow birch

14. *Fomitopsis betulina*
    birch polypore fungus

15. *Monotropa uniflora*
    ghost flower

16. *Trillium undulatum*
    painted trillium

for foraging mammals and pollinating insects. In the rich ground layer, we find red trillium (*Trillium erectum*), trout-lily (*Erythronium americanum*), bloodroot (*Sanguinaria canadensis*), false Solomon's seal (*Maianthemum racemosum*), and red baneberry (*Actaea rubra*). The deciduous woodland also supports a profusion of ferns like the delicate maidenhair fern (*Adiantum pedatum*) (17) and the ostrich fern (*Matteuccia struthiopteris*), which gives us delicious fiddleheads in the spring.

Mixed Woodlands are also prevalent, where broad-leaved trees such as yellow birch (*Betula alleghaniensis*) combine with coniferous species like eastern hemlock (*Tsuga canadensis*), creating variable light conditions. With wild sarsaparilla (*Aralia nudicaulis*) we find a wide variety of ground-layer plants, including wild lily-of-the-valley (*Maianthemum canadense*), bunch-berry (*Cornus canadensis*) (18), bluebead lily (*Clintonia borealis*), the large-leaved aster (*Eurybia macrophylla*), and shinleaf (*Pyrola elliptica*), which has beautiful nodding white waxy flowers and gained its name from its use as an analgesic for bruised shins.

Typical on alkaline soils, the Calcareous Woodland habitat supports red oak (*Quercus rubra*), white ash (*Fraxinus americana*), and sugar maple (*Acer saccharum*), with an understorey of the bright-red stems of red osier dogwood (*Swidea sericea*) and soapberry (*Shepherdia canadensis*). In the ground layer, we can see the colourful Canada goldenrod (*Solidago canadensis*), a great source of nectar and pollen for bees, shrubby cinquefoil (*Dasiphora fruticosa*), Canada anemone (*Anemonastrum canadense*), the bird's-eye primrose (*Primula laurentiana*), and the lovely and uncommon orchid, yellow lady's-slipper (*Cypripedium parviflorum*) (19).

Trees tolerant of damp conditions in Wet Woodlands include red maple (*Acer rubrum*), black spruce (*Picea mariana*), eastern white cedar (*Thuja occidentalis*), and bur oak (*Quercus macrocarpa*). Understorey species, including moose maple (*Acer pensylvanicum*) and grey alder (*Alnus incana*), offer summer shade to a profusion of ferns. The interrupted fern (*Osmunda claytoniana*), so called because of the gaps in its blades where sporulating fronds wither and

17. *Adiantum pedatum*
maidenhair fern

18. *Cornus canadensis*
bunchberry

19. *Cypripedium parviflorum*
yellow lady's-slipper

20. *Osmundastrum cinnamomeum*
    cinnamon fern

21. *Setophaga palmarum*
    palm warbler and
    *Larix laricina*
    larch

21.

drop off, cinnamon fern (*Osmundastrum cinnamomeum*) (20), with its erect central cinnamon-coloured fertile fronds, and the sensitive fern (*Onoclea sensibilis*), which is the first to brown off in fall frosts, are all wet-site specialists. Sphagnum mosses (*Sphagnum* spp.) also love damp conditions, along with jack-in-the-pulpit (*Arisaema triphyllum*), the white turtlehead (*Chelone glabra*), winterberry (*Ilex verticillata*), meadow rue (*Thalictrum pubescens*), horsetails (*Equisetum* spp.), and the beautiful rhodora (*Rhododendron canadense*), to which Ralph Waldo Emerson (1803-1882) wrote an ode. The Wet Woodland garden is kept moist by deliberate leakage over the stream clay liner and contributes to the streamside marginal habitat.

## The Stream

The meandering Stream runs through the entire southern side of the botanical gardens, creating the sight and sounds of a babbling brook, with shady pools and light-filled riffles. Bridges and stepping stones allow crossing and recrossing through the streamside habitats (22, 23), and a waterfall halfway down adds noise, splash, and spray to the experience. The streamy sections become almost choked with the trailing roots of jewelweed (*Impatiens capensis*), which has to be cut back annually to keep it in check. Bright marsh marigolds (*Caltha palustris*), the showy Canada lily (*Lilium canadense*), swamp milkweed (*Asclepias incarnata*), and water arum (*Calla palustris*) line the banks, and fragrant meadowsweet (*Spiraea alba*) and meadow rue (*Thalictrum pubescens*) thrive in the damp margins. Clumps of sensitive fern (*Onoclea sensibilis*) grow among the mossy rocks. As you watch dragonflies (*Odonata* spp.) hunting across the water, it is hard to believe that the Stream is not natural but rather an artifice relying on hidden pumps and pipework.

23.

## The Bog Garden

The Bog Garden is home to an amazing variety of specialist plants adapted to the poor, wet, acidic, peaty soils and open, light conditions (24). Sphagnum mosses (*Sphagnum* spp.), of which there are many types, predominate, with leathery-leafed sub-shrubs like leatherleaf (*Chamaedaphne calyculata*) (25), sheep laurel (*Kalmia angustifolia*) (26), bog laurel (*Kalmia polifolia*), large cranberry (*Vaccinium macrocarpon*) (27), and bog huckleberry (*Gaylussacia bigeloviana*). Most intriguing are the carnivorous plants such as the pitcher plant (*Sarracenia purpurea*) (28), the floral emblem of Newfoundland and Labrador, which drowns insects in its pitcher-like flower, and the round-leaved sundew (*Drosera rotundifolia*) (29), which traps them in its sticky tentacles. Both survive this nutrient-deficient environment by extracting ammonia from the insects' bodies to replace the nitrogen lacking in the soil. Orchids thrive here, and we can spot rose pogonia (*Pogonia ophioglossoides*) (30), white-fringed orchid (*Platanthera blephariglottis*), and grass-pink orchid (*Calopogon tuberosus*). Bunchberry (*Cornus canadensis*), starflower (*Trientalis borealis*), and wintergreen (*Gaultheria procumbens*), all of which we see in the damp acid parts of coniferous woodland, also grow here, along with rushes and sedges such as the white beakrush (*Rhynchospora alba*) and cottongrasses (*Eriophorum* spp.), and many liverworts and lichens.

Mirroring what can often happen in the wild, the Bog community gradually dried out and became less diverse. This was probably from an unwanted supply of nutrient from surrounding areas, leading to overgrowth of water-demanding plants, combined with a leaky clay liner. As we write, the leakage has been corrected and a fresh area of bog has been transplanted, with improved peripheral cut-off drains to prevent runoff from surrounding areas.

25.

25. *Chamaedaphne calyculata*
    leatherleaf

26. *Kalmia angustifolia*
    sheep laurel

27. *Vaccinium macrocarpon*
    large cranberry

28. *Sarracenia purpurea*
pitcher plant

29. *Drosera rotundifolia*
round-leaved sundew

30. *Pogonia ophioglossoides*
rose pogonia

# The Sand Barrens

The Annapolis Valley Sand Barrens are one of the rarest and most endangered habitats in the Acadian Forest Region (31). They are typified by well-drained, sandy, acidic soils formed when melting glaciers left outwash deposits. Dependent on fire to burn off shade-creating tree and shrub growth for their ecological stability, the open, bare areas support fire-adapted plants, such as rapidly regrowing rhizomatous species like bracken fern (*Pteridium aquilinum*) and sweet-fern (*Comptonia peregrina*), or sparse deeper-rooted trees such as jack pine (*Pinus banksiana*) (32) and red pine (*Pinus resinosa*). Pioneer species, quickest to re-establish from seed, include trembling aspen (*Populus tremuloides*) and grey birch (*Betula populifolia*) (33). Broom-crowberry (*Corema conradii*), a member of the heath family, enlists the help of ants who bury its seeds, which then germinate after fire. Dwarf shrubs such as lowbush blueberry (*Vaccinium angustifolium*), bearberry (*Arctostaphylos uva-ursi*) (34), and heath-like hudsonia (*Hudsonia ericoides*) and the herbaceous perennial pussytoes (*Antennaria neglecta*) also survive in the poor, dry soils. This area of the garden is one of the hardest to maintain in anything like a natural state, needing constant work to emulate the after-effects of a fire by clearing the ground and thinning shrubs and trees before they can create shade, or return too much nutrient to the soil with leaf litter.

**31.** The Sand Barrens

**32.** *Pinus banksiana*
jack pine

**33.** *Betula populifolia*
grey birch

**34.** *Arctostaphylos uva-ursi*
common bearberry

32.

34.

33.

35.

## The Freshwater Inland Marsh

By controlling water levels, we can emulate spring freshet conditions to support a range of aquatic and marginal species, which tolerate seasonal flooding but also like to dry out a bit in the summer in full sun (35). Common arrowhead (*Sagittaria latifolia*) (37) and common cattail or broadleaf cattail (*Typha latifolia*) (38) fringe the area of deeper water, preferred by the fragrant water-lily (*Nymphaea odorata*) and pickerelweed (*Pontederia cordata*). The banks are also colonized by yellow avens (*Geum aleppicum*), marsh marigold (*Caltha palustris*) (39), and swamp rose (*Rosa palustris*) (36). Wildfowl are frequent visitors to marshes, and a pair of mallards visit the gardens every spring. A drystone wall with a turf cap acts as a backdrop to the Freshwater Inland Marsh, an interesting feature and a home for invertebrates over the winter.

36.

35. Bird's-eye view of the Freshwater Marsh

36. *Rosa palustris* swamp rose

37. *Sagittaria latifolia* common arrowhead

38. *Typha latifolia*
   broadleaf cattail

39. *Caltha palustris*
   marsh marigold

   (clockwise from top right) Male mallard, painted turtle, and damselfly

## Old Field Meadow

An area of existing old meadow was transplanted to an open area in the gardens by taking deep turfs so as to include deep-rooted plants and preserve soil mycorrhizae. This creates an ideal transition between the neatly mown formal lawns and the wildness of the woodland edge. This is a plagioclimatic habitat — one in which the influences of humans have prevented further successional evolution (to scrubland and ultimately woodland in this case). Old meadows rely on grazing animals or mowing to maintain their balance and diversity. They are adversely affected by nutrient release (plowing or artificial fertilizer), which disturbs soil mycorrhizae and encourages rank grass and ruderal weed growth that can shade out sun-loving native species like red fescue (*Festuca rubra*) and oatgrass (*Danthonia spicata*), wild strawberry (*Fragaria virginiana*), smooth rose (*Rosa blanda*), common yarrow (*Achillea millefolium*), and rough fleabane (*Erigeron strigosus*). We also see non-native species such as cuckoo flower or lady's smock (*Cardamine pratensis*), red clover (*Trifolium pratense*), yellow goatsbeard (*Tragopogon pratensis*), wild carrot (*Daucus carota*) (40), and vetch (*Vicia cracca*). Though now common in the region, these are introductions from Europe. Lupins (*Lupinus polyphyllus*), now widespread, are native to western Canada and probably migrated east in gardens and animal feedstuffs. The question arises: do we try to eradicate these incomers in an attempt to maintain a "pure" Old Field Meadow, or do we accept them as naturalized plants that have become an integral part of the meadow and are of value to pollinators? The answer seems to be a matter of balance: if the non-native plants contribute as part of an integral mix, that is one thing; if they are invasive and threaten the native plants, that is quite another. Like the Bog Garden, the Old Field Meadow demonstrates the fragility of endangered habitats in the modern world. It is an increasingly rare habitat.

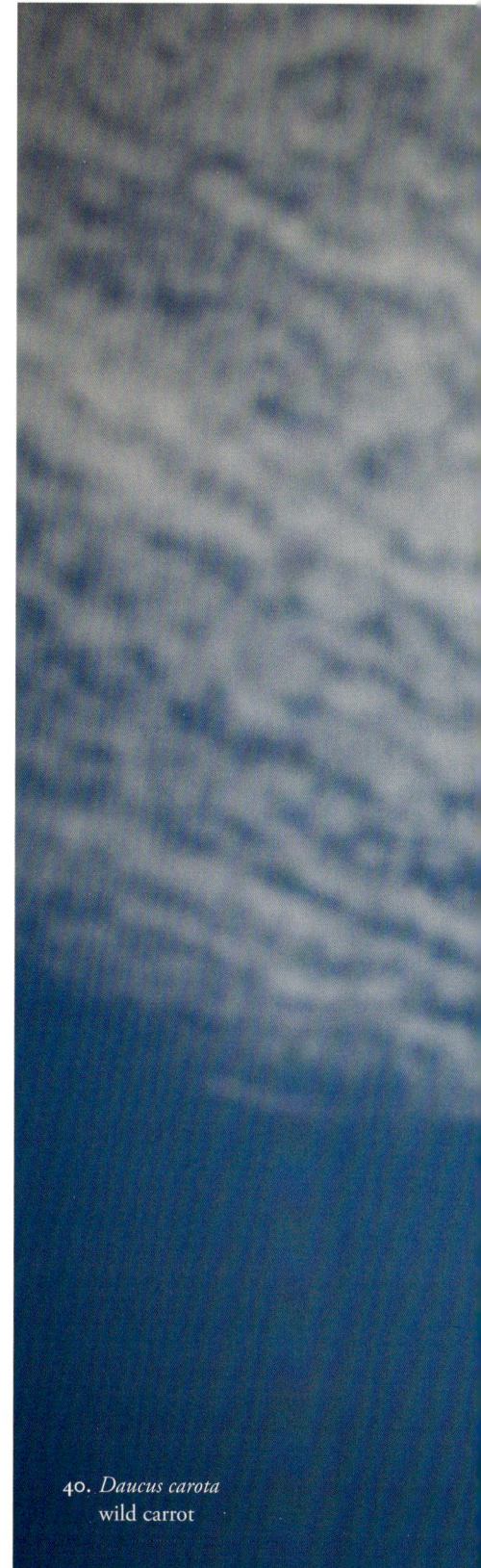

40. *Daucus carota*
wild carrot

## The Herbaceous Bank

In constructing the Quiet Lawn, we were left with a southwest-facing bank, and the opportunity was taken to make a collection of native flowering plants that enjoy an open, sunny aspect (41). They are not all found together in the wild, so this is more of a traditional herbaceous border with wildflowers than a habitat type. Tall spikes of blue lobelia (*Lobelia siphilitica*) (42) and sprays of yellow cut-leaved coneflower (*Rudbeckia laciniata*), white turtlehead (*Chelone glabra*), and purple Joe-Pye weed (*Eutrochium maculatum*) jostle with lilac-coloured wild bergamot (*Monarda fistulosa*), hairy beardtongue (*Penstemon hirsutus*), pink swamp milkweed (*Asclepias incarnata*) (43, 44), and bright-orange butterfly milkweed (*Asclepias tuberosa*) (45) in a riot of midsummer colour. The Herbaceous Bank is an important source of nectar and pollen in the gardens for pollinating insects.

42. *Lobelia siphilitica*
    *blue lobelia*

43. *Asclepias incarnata*
    swamp milkweed

44. *Asclepias incarnata*
    swamp milkweed seeds

42.

43.

44.

**45.** *Asclepias tuberosa*
butterfly milkweed (background)
*Anaphalis margaritacea*
pearly everlasting (foreground)

## The Coastal Headlands

We built rock and gravel ledges into a south-facing bank overlooking the Quiet Lawn to emulate the exposed, rocky conditions of coastal headlands. The collection of plants is chosen from those adapted to conserving moisture and withstanding harsh, abrasive, salt-laden winds: stocky plants with thick, stiff leaves like bayberry (*Morella pensylvanica*) and black crowberry (*Empetrum nigrum*) (46). The needles of low-growing conifers such as common juniper (*Juniperus communis*) and creeping juniper (*Juniperus horizontalis*) are also good at resisting drought and desiccation. Other tough plants that like rocky places include harebell (*Campanula rotundifolia*), blue-eyed grass (*Sisyrinchium montanum*) (47), three-toothed cinquefoil (*Sibbaldiopsis tridentata*) (48), and the fleshy stonecrop roseroot (*Rhodiola rosea*).

46.

**46.** *Empetrum nigrum*
black crowberry

**47.** *Sisyrinchium montanum*
blue-eyed grass

**48.** *Sibbaldiopsis tridentata*
three-toothed cinquefoil

47.

48.

# The Medicinal and Food Plant Garden

Laid out in regular beds on either side of a pleached Linden Walk within a sheltering hedge of eastern white cedar (*Thuja occidentalis*), this collection is part ornamental garden feature on the circular garden route and part educational resource. Frequently, parties of schoolchildren busily sketch the plants and make notes from the information boards (49). Some plants are native to the region, used by the Wabanaki in their traditional medicines, and some were introduced from Europe and Eurasia by early settlers, such as arnica (*Arnica montana*) (50). Examples of the native plants include American sweetflag (*Acorus americanus*) (51), a tall wetland monocotyledon traditionally used to treat digestive disorders; fireweed or great willow herb (*Chamaenerion angustifolium*), a showy perennial that quickly colonizes fire sites, clearings, and riverbanks, the young leaves of which are a good source of vitamin C and pro-vitamin A; and the may-apple (*Podophyllum peltatum*), a spreading rhizomatous plant with nodding white flowers, used as an emetic, cathartic, and treatment for gut parasites (anthelmintic). Blue vervain (*Verbena hastata*) (52), a hardy and drought-resistant plant, was used to make remedies for sore throats and respiratory tract disorders, while sweetgrass (*Anthoxanthum nitens*), a plant of salt marshes, contains coumarin, known to be an antimicrobial, antiviral, and anti-inflammatory agent.

49.

**49.** Learning at Kids Camp

**50.** *Arnica montana*
arnica

**51.** *Acorus americanus*
American sweetflag

**52.** *Verbena hastata*
blue vervain

50.

52.

51.

Of the introduced species, marsh-mallow (*Althea officinalis*) (53) was used as a food plant but also in traditional medicine for irritation of the mouth, throat, and stomach (*Althea* is derived from the Greek "to cure"). Arnica (*Arnica montana*) is still well known for its analgesic properties, especially for bruises. It is a member of the sunflower family (*Asteraceae*) and has an abundance of yellow daisy flowers in high summer. Other members of this family with healing properties in the collection include purple coneflower (*Echinacea purpurea*), elecampane or horseheal (*Inula helenium*), and edelweiss (*Leontopodium alpinum*). Echinacea is said to stimulate the immune system and reduce the symptoms of colds and flu; elecampane root is a cough suppressant and expectorant; and edelweiss, the symbol of purity in alpine countries, is known to help gastrointestinal complaints and ease rheumatic pain.

This educational space, while formally laid out in a grid for classification and learning, provides a pleasant and contemplative stroll (54, 55).

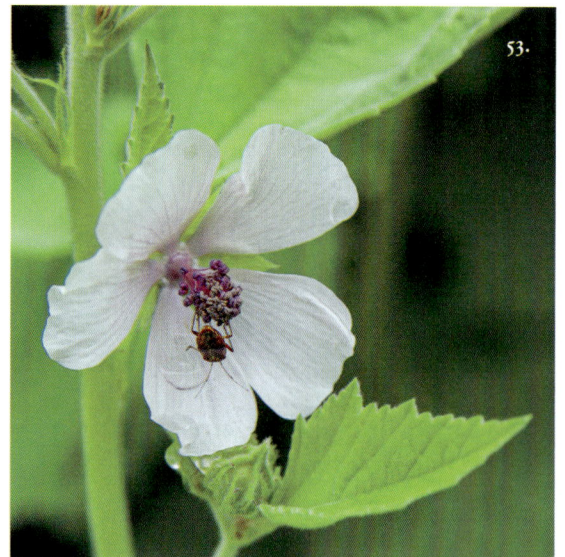

53. *Althea officinalis*
marsh-mallow

54. Aerial view of the formal pathway

55. The Linden Walk

*Echinacea purpurea*
purple coneflower

# APPENDIX

This appendix presents a selection of plants found in the Harriet Irving Botanical Gardens.
It is organized by Latin name, followed by the plant's common name, its location
in the gardens, and its natural habitat in the Acadian Forest region.

1.  *Abies balsamea*
    balsam fir
    Coniferous Woodland
    upland forests and swamps

2.  *Acer rubrum*
    red maple
    Wet Woodland
    upland forests and swamps

3.  *Acer saccharum*
    sugar maple
    Deciduous Woodland
    nutrient-rich upland forests

4.  *Achillea millefolium*
    common yarrrow
    Meadow
    open dry grassy areas

5.  *Acorus americanus*
    American sweetflag
    Medicinal Garden
    marshes and freshwater shores

6. *Actaea rubra*
   red baneberry
   Deciduous Woodland
   upland and floodplain forests

7. *Adiantum pedatum*
   northern maidenhair fern
   Deciduous Woodland
   nutrient-rich upland and
   floodplain forests

8. *Alnus alnobetula ssp. Crispa*
   green alder
   Freshwater Inland Marsh
   swamps and moist disturbed areas

9. *Althaea officinalis*
   marsh-mallow
   Medicinal Garden
   not native to Acadian Forest
   Region

10. *Amelanchier canadensis*
    serviceberry
    Walled Garden
    upland forest edges and openings

11. *Andromeda polifolia*
    bog rosemary
    Bog Garden
    bogs and fens

12. *Anemonastrum canadense*
    Canada anemone
    Calcareous Woodland
    freshwater shorelines and forest
    openings

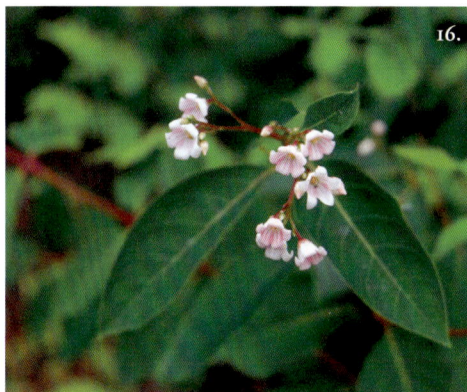

13. *Antennaria neglecta*
field pussytoes
Sand Barrens
open dry areas

14. *Anthoxanthum nitens*
sweetgrass
Medicinal Garden
salt marshes and river shores

15. *Apios americana*
American ground-nut
Stream
freshwater shores

16. *Apocynum androsaemifolium*
spreading dogbane
Sand Barrens
upland forest edges and openings

17. *Aquilegia canadensis*
red columbine
Herbaceous Bank
rocky slopes and river shores

18. *Aralia nudicaulis*
wild sarsaparilla
Mixed Woodland
forests

19. *Arctostaphylos uva-ursi*
    common bearberry
    Sand Barrens
    open dry areas

20. *Arisaema triphyllum*
    jack-in-the-pulpit
    Wet Woodland
    nutrient-rich moist to wet forests

21. *Arnica montana*
    arnica
    Medicinal Garden
    not native to Acadian Forest
    Region

22. *Asclepias incarnata*
    swamp milkweed
    Herbaceous Bank
    fens and swamps

23  *Asclepias tuberosa*
    butterfly milkweed
    Herbaceous Bank
    open dry areas

24. *Betula alleghaniensis*
    yellow birch
    Mixed Woodland
    forests and swamps

25. *Betula populifolia*
grey birch
Sand Barrens
forests and open dry areas

26. *Calla palustris*
water arum
Stream
swamps and marshes

27. *Caltha palustris*
marsh marigold
Stream
swamps and floodplains

28. *Campanula rotundifolia*
harebell
Coastal Headlands
rocky ledges

29. *Cardamine pratensis*
cuckoo flower
Meadow
not native to Acadian Forest
Region

30. *Caulophyllum thalictroides*
blue cohosh
Deciduous Woodland
nutrient-rich upland and
floodplain forests

31. *Chamaedaphne calyculata*
leatherleaf
Bog Garden
open wetlands and freshwater
shores

32. *Chamaenerion angustifolium*
    fireweed
    Medicinal Garden
    forest edges and openings

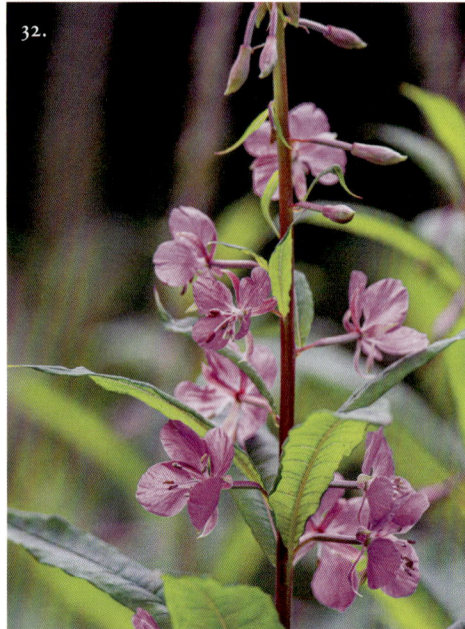

33. *Chelone glabra*
    turtlehead
    Wet Woodland
    swamps and freshwater shores

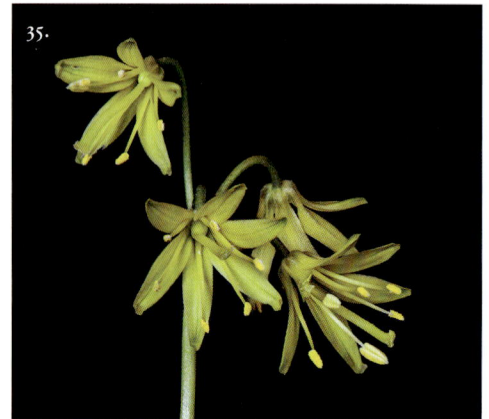

34. *Claytonia caroliniana*
    spring beauty
    Herbaceous Bank
    nutrient-rich upland forests

35. *Clintonia borealis*
    bluebead lily
    Mixed Woodland
    forests

36. *Comptonia peregrina*
    sweet-fern
    Sand Barrens
    open dry areas

37. *Coptis trifolia*
    goldthread
    Coniferous Woodland
    forests

38. *Corema conradii*
    broom crowberry
    Coastal Headlands
    open dry areas

39. *Cornus canadensis*
    bunchberry
    Mixed Woodland
    forests

40. *Corylus cornuta*
    beaked hazelnut
    Deciduous Woodland
    nutrient-rich upland forests and
    forest edges

41. *Crocanthemum canadense*
    frostweed
    Experimental Garden
    open dry areas

42. *Cypripedium acaule*
    pink lady's-slipper
    Coniferous Woodland
    forests

43. *Cypripedium parviflorum*
    yellow lady's-slipper
    Calcareous Woodland
    nutrient-rich forests

44. *Cypripedium reginae*
showy lady's-slipper
Wet Woodland
nutrient-rich swamps

45. *Dasiphora fruticosa*
shrubby cinquefoil
Calcareous Woodland
open nutrient-rich areas

46. *Diervilla lonicera*
nothern bush-honeysuckle
Walled Garden
forest edges and openings

47. *Drosera filiformis*
thread-leaved sundew
Bog Garden
bogs

48. *Drosera rotundifolia*
round-leaved sundew
Bog Garden
open wetlands and freshwater
shores

49. *Echinacea purpurea*
eastern purple coneflower
Medicinal Garden
not native to Acadian Forest
Region

50. *Epigaea repens*
mayflower
Walled Garden
forests and forest edges

51. *Equisetum arvense*
    field horsetail
    Wet Woodland
    open areas and floodplains

52. *Erigeron strigosus*
    rough fleabane
    Meadow
    open dry areas

53. *Erythronium americanum*
    yellow trout-lily
    Deciduous Woodland
    nutrient-rich upland and
    floodplain forests

54. *Eurybia macrophylla*
    large-leaved aster
    Mixed Woodland
    forests

55. *Eutrochium maculatum*
    Joe-Pye weed
    Stream
    marshes and swamps

56. *Fagus grandifolia*
    American beech
    Deciduous Woodland
    upland forests

57. *Fragaria virginiana*
    wild strawberry
    Meadow
    open dry areas

58. *Fraxinus americana*
    white ash
    Experimental Garden
    nutrient-rich upland forests and
    swamps

59. *Fraxinus nigra*
    black ash
    Experimental Garden
    swamps and floodplains

60. *Gaultheria procumbens*
    wintergreen
    Coniferous Woodland
    forests

61. *Geranium maculatum*
    spotted geranium
    Freshwater Inland Marsh
    forest edges and freshwater shores

62. *Geum aleppicum*
    yellow avens
    Freshwater Inland Marsh
    floodplain forests and swamps

63. *Geum peckii*
eastern mountain avens
Experimental Garden
alpine or maritime fens and
seepages

64. *Geum rivale*
water avens
Herbaceous Bank
swamps

65. *Houstonia caerulea*
bluets
Walled Garden
open dry areas

66. *Hudsonia ericoides*
hudsonia
Sand Barrens
open dry areas

67. *Hydrocotyle umbellata*
water pennywort
Experimental Garden
freshwater shores

68. *Ilex glabra*
inkberry
Walled Garden
bogs and moist upland forests

69. *Ilex verticillata*
winterberry
Wet Woodland
swamps and fens

70. *Impatiens capensis*
spotted jewelweed
Freshwater Inland Marsh
swamps and forests

71. *Inula helenium*
elecampane
Medicinal Garden
not native to Acadian Forest
Region

72. *Iris versicolor*
blue flag
Stream
freshwater shores and swamps

73. *Juniperus communis*
common juniper
Coastal Headlands
open dry areas

74. *Juniperus horizontalis*
creeping juniper
Coastal Headlands
nutrient-rich open dry areas

75. *Kalmia angustifolia*
sheep laurel
Bog Garden
bogs and upland forests

76. *Laportea canadensis*
    Canada wood nettle
    Experimental Garden
    nutrient-rich floodplain and
    upland forests

77. *Larix laricina*
    larch
    Coniferous Woodland
    bogs and fens

78. *Lemna turionifera*
    turion duckweed
    Freshwater Inland Marsh
    marshes

79. *Leontopodium alpinum*
    edelweiss
    Medicinal Garden
    not native to Acadian Forest
    Region

80. *Leucanthemum vulgare*
    oxeye daisy
    Meadow
    not native to Acadian Forest
    Region

81. *Lilium canadense*
    Canada lily
    Experimental Garden
    floodplain forests and freshwater
    shores

82. *Lobelia cardinalis*
cardinal flower
Walled Garden
freshwater shores

83. *Lobelia siphilitica*
great blue lobelia
Herbaceous Bank
marshes and freshwater shores

84. *Lonicera canadensis*
fly-honeysuckle
Deciduous Woodland
upland forests

85. *Lupinus polyphyllus*
lupin
Meadow
not native to Acadian Forest
Region

86. *Lysimachia borealis*
starflower
Coniferous Woodland
forests

87. *Lysimachia terrestris*
swamp candles
Coastal Headlands
swamps and marshes

88. *Maianthemum canadense*
wild lily-of-the-valley
Mixed Woodland
forests

89. *Maianthemum racemosum*
false Solomon's seal
Deciduous Woodland
nutrient-rich forests and
floodplains

90. *Mitchella repens*
partridgeberry
Mixed Woodland
forests

91. *Monarda fistulosa*
wild bergamot
Herbaceous Bank
forests and forest openings

92. *Monotropa uniflora*
ghost flower
Coniferous Woodland
forests

93. *Morella pensylvanica*
northern bayberry
Coastal Headlands
open dry to moist areas

94. *Nymphaea odorata*
fragrant water-lily
Freshwater Inland Marsh
freshwater marshes

95. *Oclemena nemoralis*
    bog aster
    Bog Garden
    bogs and freshwater shores

96. *Onoclea sensibilis*
    sensitive fern
    Wet Woodland
    swamps and freshwater shores

97. *Osmunda claytoniana*
    interrupted fern
    Wet Woodland
    moist forests and forest edges

98. *Osmunda regalis*
    royal fern
    Stream
    swamps and freshwater shores

99. *Osmundastrum cinnamomeum*
    cinnamon fern
    Wet Woodland
    swamps

100. *Ostrya virginiana*
    iron wood
    Calcareous Woodland
    nutrient-rich upland and
    floodplain forests

101. *Penstemon hirsutus*
    hairy beardtongue
    Herbaceous Bank
    open dry areas

102. *Picea mariana*
    black spruce
    Bog Garden
    bogs and upland forests

103. *Picea rubens*
    red spruce
    Coniferous Woodland
    forests

104. *Pinus banksiana*
    jack pine
    Sand Barrens
    forests and forest openings

105. *Pinus resinosa*
    red pine
    Sand Barrens
    forests and open dry areas

106. *Pinus strobus*
     eastern white pine
     Coniferous Woodland
     forests

107. *Podophyllum peltatum*
     may-apple
     Medicinal Garden
     forest edges and meadows

108. *Pogonia ophioglossoides*
     rose pogonia
     Bog Garden
     bogs and freshwater shores

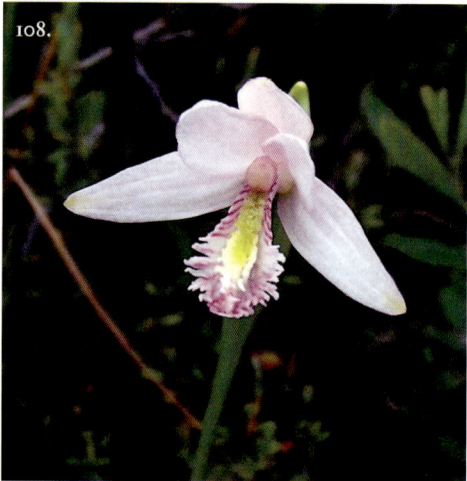

109. *Polystichum acrostichoides*
     Christmas fern
     Walled Garden
     nutrient-rich upland forests

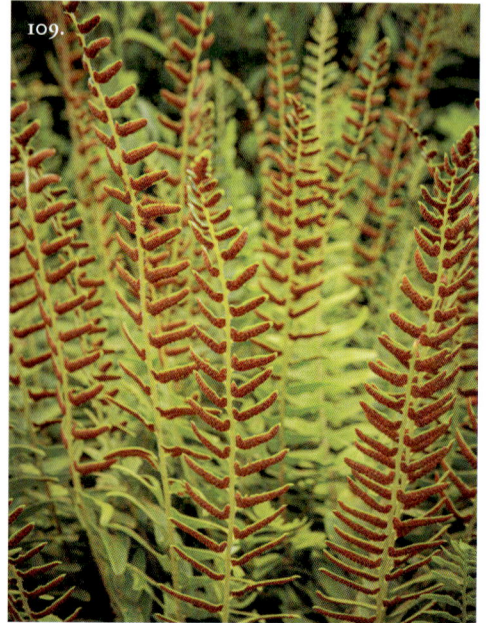

110. *Pontederia cordata*
     pickerelweed
     Freshwater Inland Marsh
     marshes and freshwater shores

111.

112.

113.

115.

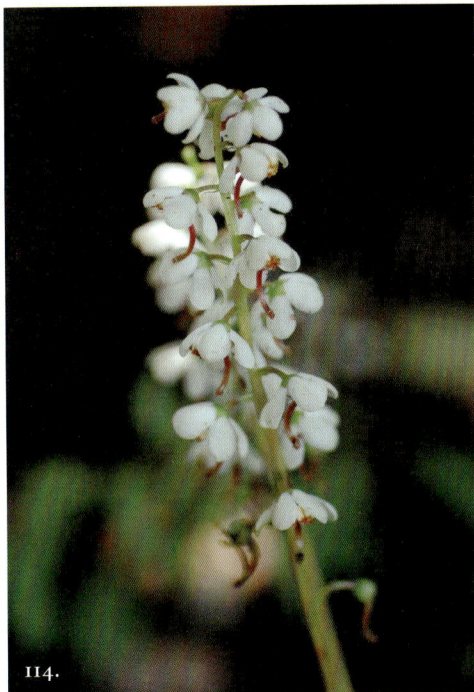

114.

111. *Populus tremuloides*
trembling aspen
Sand Barrens
early successional forests

112. *Primula laurentiana*
bird's-eye primrose
Calcareous Woodland
rocky ledges

113. *Pteridium aquilinum*
bracken fern
Calcareous Woodland
forests and forest openings

114. *Pyrola elliptica*
shinleaf
Mixed Woodland
upland forests

115. *Quercus rubra*
red oak
Calcareous Woodland
upland forests

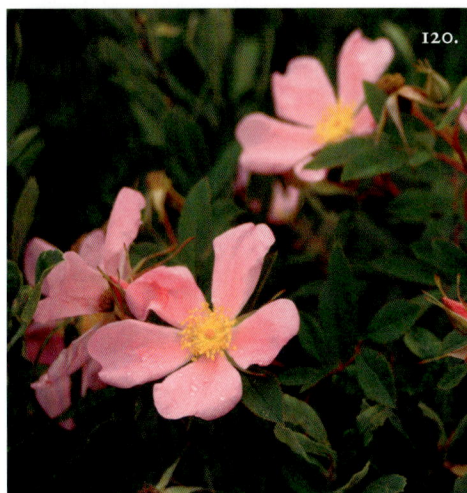

116. *Ranunculus acris*
tall buttercup
Meadow
not native to Acadian Forest Region

117. *Rhodiola rosea*
roseroot
Coastal Headlands
rocky ledges

118. *Rhus typhina*
staghorn sumac
Mixed Woodland
open dry areas and forest edges

119. *Rosa blanda*
smooth rose
Meadow
freshwater shores

120. *Rosa palustris*
swamp rose
Freshwater Inland Marsh
fens and freshwater shores

121. *Rosa virginiana*
Virginia rose
Walled Garden
open dry to moist areas

122. *Rudbeckia laciniata*
cut-leaved coneflower
Herbaceous Bank
floodplains and freshwater shores

123. *Sagittaria latifolia*
common arrowhead
Freshwater Inland Marsh
marshes and freshwater shores

124. *Sambucus canadensis*
common elderberry
Stream
open wetlands and freshwater
shores

125. *Sanguinaria canadensis*
bloodroot
Experimental Garden
nutrient-rich floodplain and
upland forests

126. *Sarracenia purpurea*
northern pitcher plant
Bog Garden
bogs and swamps

127. *Shepherdia canadensis*
soapberry
Calcareous Woodland
nutrient-rich open dry areas

128. *Sibbaldiopsis tridentata*
three-toothed cinquefoil
Coastal Headlands
open dry areas

129. *Sisyrinchium montanum*
blue-eyed-grass
Coastal Headlands
open dry areas

130. *Sium suave*
common water-parsnip
Stream
marshes and shorelines of rivers
and lakes

131. *Solidago sempervirens*
seaside goldenrod
Coastal Headlands
coastal beaches

132. *Spiraea alba*
meadowsweet
Stream
forest edges and openings

133. *Swida sericea*
red-osier dogwood
Calcareous Woodland
wetlands and forest edges

134. *Symphyotrichum cordifolium*
heart-leaved aster
Walled Garden
forest edges and openings

135. *Symphyotrichum novi-belgii*
New York aster
Walled Garden
forest edges and openings

136. *Thalictrum pubescens*
tall meadow-rue
Stream
salt marshes and open dry areas

137. *Thuja occidentalis*
eastern white cedar
Calcareous Woodland
swamps and freshwater shores

138. *Trifolium pratense*
red clover
Meadow
not native to Acadian Forest
Region

139. *Trillium erectum*
red trillium
Deciduous Woodland
nutrient-rich upland forests

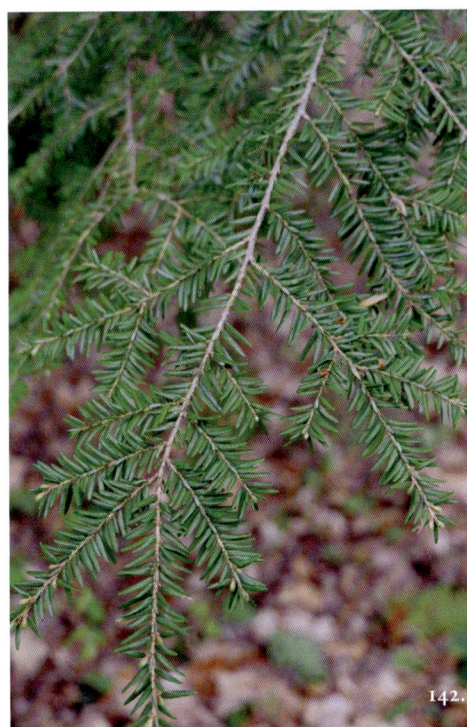

140. *Trillium undulatum*
painted trillium
Coniferous Woodland
forests

141. *Triosteum aurantiacum*
orange-fruit horse-gentian
Experimental Garden
upland and floodplain forests and
forest edges

142. *Tsuga canadensis*
eastern hemlock
Mixed Woodland
forests

143. *Typha latifolia*
broadleaf cattail
Freshwater Inland Marsh
marshes

144. *Vaccinium angustifolium*
lowbush blueberry
Sand Barrens
forests and open dry areas

145. *Vaccinium corymbosum*
highbush blueberry
Experimental Garden
swamps and freshwater shores

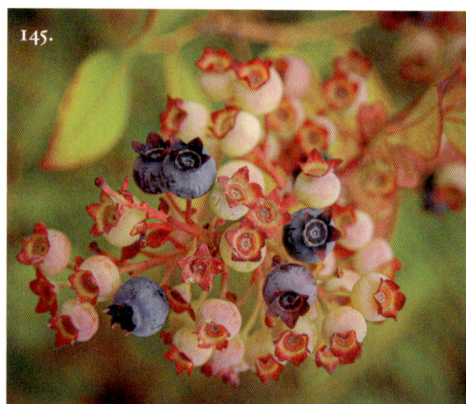

146. *Vaccinium macrocarpon*
large cranberry
Bog Garden
bogs and freshwater shores

147. *Verbena hastata*
blue vervain
Medicinal Garden
open river floodplains

148. *Viburnum cassinoides*
witherod
Wet Woodland
forests and swamps

149. *Vicia cracca*
tufted vetch
Meadow
not native to Acadian Forest
Region

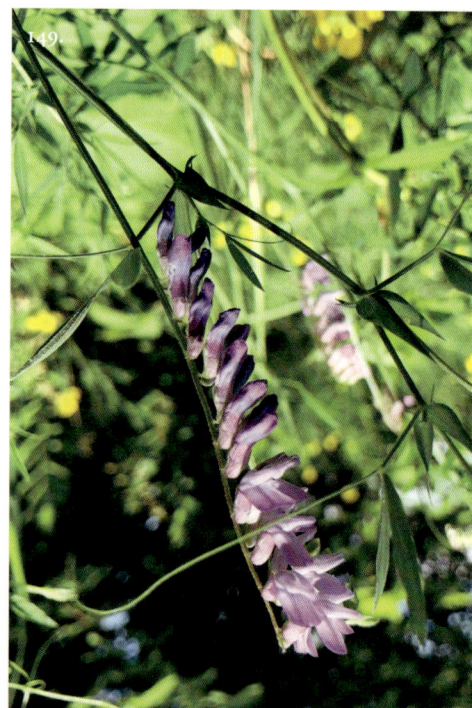

150. *Zizia aurea*
golden zizia
Herbaceous Bank
floodplains and freshwater shores

# Acknowledgements

## ALEX NOVELL

Over the twenty years since the completion of the K.C. Irving Environmental Science Centre and Harriet Irving Botanical Gardens, I have revisited many times to see the building mellow and the gardens blossom and grow. During these visits, I have often reflected on just what a Herculean effort it was by all concerned. I am grateful now to have an opportunity to acknowledge all those who were part of this project, as well as those who have helped to record its evolution in this book.

Firstly, my unending gratitude to Arthur Irving, OC, ONB, long-time friend and mentor, whose brilliant idea this was, and to whose mother and father the finished result is dedicated. Colleagues still remember his kindly advice at the very beginning, as they were about to set off into the wilds of Atlantic Canada on a research trip: "If you ever get into any kind of trouble, you must walk into the nearest Irving Station and tell them I sent you." Equally to Sandra Irving, CM, one of the most caring people I know, and one who has done so much to help others achieve academic excellence and scientific progress. Together, their boundless drive and unstinting generosity have made the idea a reality.

And to Hans Klohn, the project director, who was befriended by K.C. Irving as a young engineer after the war, who gave me such clear and helpful guidance over many years, to whom everything was achievable, and who kept us all on the straight and narrow in this undertaking.

Many talented people have contributed help, advice, and hard work over the four and a half years it took to plan, design, and build this project. I would like to express my heartfelt appreciation and gratitude to them all. Here are the ones I particularly remember, and if I have left anyone out, it does not diminish your contribution but is merely a reflection of my failing memory. Some are sadly no longer with us, but their memory lives on, not least in their work.

Kelvin Ogilvie, CM, then president of Acadia University, whose friendship, enthusiasm, and support helped to incorporate the K.C. Irving Environmental Science Centre and Harriet Irving Botanical Gardens seamlessly into the academic program.

Alex Novell and Arthur Irving

My erstwhile colleagues at Novell Tullett, who were responsible for the master plan, research, detailed design, and supervision of the making of the Gardens, including Paul Tullett, who kept the ship afloat during my long absences; Peter Richards, project landscape architect and designer extraordinaire, ably assisted by Janet Smith, Ian Richardson, and Simon Andrews in particular; also Jane Fowles, who has kindly dug into the archives to provide material for this book.

Bob Stern, Graham Wyatt, and Preston Gumberich of Robert A.M. Stern Architects, the easiest of comrades in arms and mind-blowingly brilliant in producing what must be the finest modern university building anywhere one cares to look. RAMSA archivist Tim Reddy was of tremendous assistance in providing archival visuals and photographs for this book.

Michael Rizzello, OBE, friend and eminent sculptor, who first introduced me to K.C. Irving and Arthur more than thirty years ago, since which time we have worked on many things together. He designed the bronze commemorative plaques to K.C. Irving and Harriet Irving in the Garden Pavilion, and the garden emblem — the mayflower of Nova Scotia, the thistle of Scotland, and the bee — without whose constant endeavour we could not sustain our crops and flowers.

Carl Blanchard, Jim Cosman, and Paul Rathburn of FCC Construction, the lead contractors, who motivated the myriad of craftsmen and trades, ensuring that they pulled together and in the same direction, completing a complex schedule in record time.

Peter Romkey, woodsman and naturalist, who provided much of the expertise in gathering plant material and practical know-how in its installation, and who went on to become director of the whole facility.

Melanie Priesnitz, who brought her botanical knowledge and experience to establishing the gardens, who has, with her team, been looking after them ever since, and who helped greatly in compiling this book. Both she and Dr. Rodger Evans took some stunning photographs of the gardens through the seasons which have helped greatly to illustrate and enliven my written descriptions.

Professor John Parker, then curator of Cambridge University Botanical Gardens, who invited us there and became a valued consultant from the beginning.

Dr. Bernard Jackson, who supervised the founding of the Memorial University of Newfoundland Botanical Gardens, and who provided kind hospitality, advice, and practical help, as did Dr. Wilf Nicholls, director.

Bill Cullinan of Garden in the Woods, Mass., Raymond Fielding, author of *The Shrubs of Nova Scotia*, and Captain Dick Steele, rhododendron breeder and plantsman, who were also very kind to our research team.

Jill Covell and Jamie Ellison of Bunchberry Nurseries, who collected native plant seed and grew them on for us, and Jacklyn Murray, who helped with the planting design for the Herbaceous Bank.

Dawn Lawrence of Wessex Ecology, who carried out the initial habitat studies for us.

At Acadia University Faculty of Biology, Ruth Newell, taxonomist, who helped us establish the new Herbarium and Seed Bank, which provided proper accommodation for, and added to, the important E.C. Smith Collection; and Alain Belliveau, Irving Biodiversity Collection Manager, for his help in compiling the appendix.

Dr. Graham Daborn and Dr. Ed Reekie both provided invaluable advice and guidance. Sam Vander Kloet, an expert in *Vacciniums*, grew the native blueberry collection for the Walled Garden. Also Drew Peck, facilities director at Acadia University, offered many acts of practical assistance.

Ben Scholten of Scholten's Landscape, with whom I have had a long and fruitful relationship in creating many parks and gardens in New Brunswick and Nova Scotia, and who will always go the extra mile for the perfect job. Also Dave Davis at Linden Landscapes.

My thanks also go to the scores of skilled artisans — stonemasons, bricklayers, carpenters, drystone wallers, fabricators, foundrymen, and master ironsmiths, whose beautiful work will outlast us all.

I am also in my co-author John Leroux's debt for his masterful project management of this book, quite in addition to his own substantial and insightful contribution. He has been stimulating to work with, and his close relationship with Goose Lane Editions has been an important asset in the book's production. And to Michael Cantwell who coordinated all our efforts and was instrumental in bringing this book to life.

Lastly, but not least, I would like to thank my dear wife, Harriette, without whose constant support and encouragement I would not have felt able to make the many trips to New Brunswick, Nova Scotia, New York, and much farther afield during the course of this project.

# PHOTO CREDITS

A project of this scope engages the talents of many individuals. Images have been supplied by the following (indicated by page number or image number):

All photographs by Rodger Evans, unless otherwise noted. Other contributors include Peter Aaron/OTTO (PA), Alain Belliveau (AB), ESTO (ES), Sarah Irving (SI), Samuel Jean (SJ), John Leroux (JL), Steve Mitchell (SM), Alex Novell/Novell Tullett (AN), Peter Oleskevich (PO), Melanie Priesnitz (MP), Robert A.M. Stern Architects (RS), Neil Setchfield/Alamy Stock Photo (NS), and Wikimedia Commons (WC).

### Foreword
(JL) p. 8; (SM) p. 10; (MP) p. 11

### Master Plan
(AB) 5; (JL) 12, 15, 17, 19, 22, 24, 26–28; (AN) 1, 2, 8, 10, 11, 13; (MP) 4; (NS) 9

### An Exceptional Balance of Form and Substance
(PA) 8–10; (ES) 19, 25, 28, 29, 31–36, 38, 41, 42; (JL) 1–6, 30, 39, 43, 44, 47, 48; (AN) 7; (PO) 40; (MP) 45; (RS) 11, 14–18, 20–24; (WC, Steve Cadman, photographer, CCBY-SA 2.0) 12; (WC, Daniel Case, photographer, CCBY-SA 3.0) 13; (WC, Dietmar Rabich, photographer, CCBY-SA 4.0) 46

### The Making of the Gardens
(ES) 2; (JL) 8; (AN) 3–5

### Habitat Types and the Choice of Plants
(AB) 33; (ES) 1; (SI) 22; (SJ) 29, 50; (JL) 4, 5, 24, 31; (AN) 41, 55; (PO) 3, 49; (MP) 2, 8, 12, 15, 18, 26, 32, 36, 39, 42, 45, 48, 51; (WC, CCBY-SA 3.0) 30; (WC, H. Zell, CC BY-SA 3.0) 46

### Appendix
(AB) 25, 37, 59, 108, 126, 130; (SJ) 21, 48, 106; (PO) 50; (MP) 5, 7, 8, 13, 14, 16, 20, 24, 28, 29, 33, 36, 40, 43, 45, 54, 61–63, 68, 69, 73, 76, 78–80, 83, 85, 91, 92, 95, 100, 102, 104, 110, 113, 114, 116–20, 122, 123, 128, 129, 131, 132, 134–38, 142, 144, 149

### Acknowledgements
(AN) 172

(Rodger Evans & Philip LeBlanc) 176

**THE GARDEN ROOM**

WHEN I WAS ASKED TO BE THE CHANCELLOR OF ACADIA UNIVERSITY,
I AGREED TO DO SO IF THERE WAS SOMETHING THAT I COULD DO FOR
THE UNIVERSITY AND ITS STUDENTS.

MY EARLIEST THOUGHT WAS TO CREATE A CAMPUS MEETING PLACE
WHERE STUDENTS, FACULTY, STAFF AND FRIENDS COULD MEET, ENJOY
EACH OTHER'S COMPANY AND FEEL VERY MUCH A PART OF ACADIA.

I HAVE MANY GOOD MEMORIES OF MY TIME AT ACADIA AS A STUDENT.
MY HOPE IS THAT YOUR STUDENT LIFE WILL BE ENHANCED BY THE
TEACHING AND RESEARCH FACILITIES AND BOTANICAL GARDENS WE
HAVE CREATED AND THAT YOU WILL BUILD MANY HAPPY MEMORIES
OF YOUR OWN HERE IN THE GARDEN ROOM.

ENJOY YOUR STAY AT ACADIA. TIME PASSES VERY QUICKLY.

*Arthur Irving*
ARTHUR IRVING